THE ART OF
STAR WARS®
GALAXY

EDITED BY GARY GERANI

DESIGNED BY ALTEMUS

TOPPS COMICS ✳ **NEW YORK**

A
C
K
N
O
W
L
E
D
G
E
M
E
N
T
S

THE ART OF STAR WARS GALAXY is published by Topps Publishing, One Whitehall Street, New York, NY 10004. TM & © 1993 Lucasfilm, Ltd. All Rights Reserved. Used Under Authorization. This book may not be reproduced in any form, without written permission of the Publisher.

Printed in Canada
First Edition: November 1993

Cover painting by Ken Steacy

10 9 8 7 6 5 4 3

Library of Congress
Cataloging-in-Publication Data

Gerani, Gary

The Art of Star Wars Galaxy: new visions of the Star Wars trilogy interpreted by comics and fantasy artists.

ISBN 1-883313-01-5

93-061430
CIP

Companies, professional groups, clubs, and other organizations may qualify for special terms when ordering quantities of this title. For information, write: Special Sales, Topps Publishing, One Whitehall Street, New York, NY 10004 or call: (212)376-0436

A limited edition of this book has been published by Underwood-Miller.

Special thanks to the folks at Lucasfilm: Howard Roffman, Julia Russo, Gary Hymowitz, Sue Rostoni, Stacy Mollema and Kathleen Scanlon. In everything from approving copy to providing stills and transparencies, these individuals were extremely efficient and understanding of our needs.

In addition, Lucasfilm Director of Publishing Lucy Wilson deserves our heartfelt appreciation for embracing our vision and providing the opportunity for this project to come to life.

Stephen J. Sansweet, Consulting Editor to the STAR WARS GALAXY card set, was also quite helpful in the development of this companion book. So was photographer Steve Essig, who shot many of the posters and illustrations used in the series. Thanks, guys!

Kudos to artist Janet Jackson for her superb coloring of numerous pencil and ink illustrations.

Design and production of this book is by Altemus Creative Servicenter, N.Y.C.

Finally, the typographical assistance of Topps staffers Claudia Canny and Sandy Fiumano is deeply appreciated.

Quotes used in the movie photo captions were derived from a number of video documentaries, movie magazines and books. (Note: page numbers refer to pages in *this* book.)

The Making of Star Wars (CBS/Fox Video, 1977)/SP FX: THE EMPIRE STRIKES BACK (CBS/Fox Video, 1980)
Pages 28, 54, 82, 114

Classic Creatures: Return of the Jedi (CBS/Fox Video, 1985)
Pages 86, 108

From Star Wars to Jedi: The Making of A Saga (CBS/Fox Company, 1986)
Pages 4, 24, 66, 74, 112

George Lucas: Heroes, Myths and Magic (American Masters/PBS, 1993)
Page 22

SCIENCE FICTION, HORROR AND FANTASY MAGAZINE (D.W. Enterprises, 1977)
Pages 32, 38, 64, 68, 96, 98, 104, 106, 108, 127

STARLOG MAGAZINE No. 13 (O'Quinn Studios, 1978)
Page 100

STARLOG MAGAZINE No. 35 (O'Quinn Studios, 1980)
Page 40, 70

THE ART OF THE EMPIRE STRIKES BACK (Ballantine Books, 1980)
Page 118

Three Ken Steacy pencil prelims for the STAR WARS GALAXY poster. The finished painting appears on our cover.

CONTENTS

A CREATIVE JOURNEY

It was art—in the form of Ralph McQuarrie's pre-production paintings—that helped sell *Star Wars* as a movie property. Before Ralph picked up his brush, no one had even seen a Wookiee or a droid. To make the films, a team of amazingly talented artists and designers had to create creatures, vehicles and environments that began only as words on a page. Art also became a significant factor in the advertising for the trilogy because each movie poster had to convey the complex moods of the films in a single painting.

Today, more than 15 years since the release of *Star Wars*, fantasy art continues to play a dynamic role in the history of the saga. On trading cards and in this book are the "New Visions" of *Star Wars*, original illustrations by top comic artists, each one offering a personal interpretation of the imagery that makes up the trilogy.

For me, it's been a gratifying creative journey that is not even halfway completed.

— *George Lucas*

Oppostie page: an unused poster painting for the original *Star Wars*, rendered by Dan Goozee with design work by Tony Seiniger and Associates.

"I think what happens in a project like *Star Wars*," observes George Lucas, "is that you fall in love with the characters. You fall in love with the environment. It's like a home...there are friends there. So there's always going to be a desire on my part to go home again–to be with my friends again."

O U R P O P H E R I T A G E

Ben (Obi-Wan) Kenobi

STAR FILE
OFFICIAL BUSINESS

Princess Leia™

CHEWBACCA™

The year was 1977. Out of nowhere, *Star Wars* blasted its way into our hearts and souls, forever changing the face of popular entertainment. For The Topps Company, then called Topps Chewing Gum, it was the beginning of an extraordinary trading card alliance that continues to this day. Creating a non-sports trading card set is very much like putting a sequential picture book together, except that the "pages" are small and

unbound. Cards based on movies traditionally offer a captioned photo on the front, with corresponding copy and a graphic of some kind on the back. When the first series of STAR WARS cards proved phenomenally successful, additional series were needed. That meant hundreds of new transparencies had to be selected and utilized. We published just about every photograph the Lucasfilm Licensing representatives had in their files. A few years later our EMPIRE and JEDI sets also spawned multiple series — and similar photo-editing marathons.

Flash forward to the present; or at least, to late 1991: The 15th Anniversary of *Star Wars* was just around the corner. Topps and Lucasfilm "wanted to do something different, some special kind of card set worthy of the saga," recalls Topps Vice President of Publishing Ira Friedman. Since I wrote and edited our original STAR WARS sets (including EMPIRE and JEDI), Ira gave me a call and asked me to develop the project.

This time, art, rather than photos, would fuel our trading card engine. I envisioned breathtaking fantasy paintings inspired by Lucas' brainchild, commissioned by Topps and rendered by the field's top illustrators. This first incarnation of STAR WARS

GALAXY was dubbed THE NEW ART OF STAR WARS, and my two-page proposal boasted the talents of Thomas Blackshear, Boris Vallejo, and John Berkey.

"That original art proposal was intriguing," remembers Friedman. "But since we were trying to get this project out by 1992, to tie in with the anniversary, we decided to go with something a little more practical." That something was intended to be another photo series, but one that would break the *Star Wars* universe into specific, focused categories — "Weapons," "Vehicles," "Planets," etc. Stephen J. Sansweet, the biggest collector of *Star Wars* merchandise and the author of a recent book on the subject, signed on as my collaborator and invaluable *Star Wars* guru.

Then a funny thing happened...

As Steve and I were preparing what we believed to be our final outline, The Topps Company gave birth to a new subsidiary, Topps Comics. Through our Editor-in-Chief Jim Salicrup, relationships had been established with some of the greatest artists in the comics field, and many of these folks were *Star Wars* fanatics thrilled to render a card for us. Overnight, the photo series became an art series again — or rather, an artful combination of just about every approach we'd been developing

and refining for the past number of months. Sure, we'd miss our '92 deadline and couldn't be classified as an "anniversary" series anymore, but we all believed that a trading card set of this caliber would be worth the wait.

Our first move was to divide the series into new categories (or "sub-sets") reinforcing our art theme. Starting things off would be "The Star Wars Ensemble," featuring a dozen character portraits by comics painter Joe Jusko (eventually replaced by

GALAXY collaborator Stephen J. Sansweet in the midst of his fabulous *Star Wars* collection, the largest in the world.

Hollywood veteran Joe Smith). The back of each card would contain a photo of the actor and a brief profile of the character he or she played.

Next up was "The Design of Star Wars," spotlighting the creations of McQuarrie, Cobb,

Various Arnie Sawyer card design experiments.

Above: a sprawling *Empire Strikes Back* painting by Jim Steranko, orignally used as a wraparound cover for his PREVUE magazine. Below: a couple of "power graphs" developed by Stephen J. Sansweet, commissioned but not used in the final series.

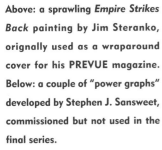

Johnston and dozens of acclaimed concept artists who worked on the trilogy. Frequently a card back would feature a photo of an alien or droid as it appeared in the movie, so one could compare it to the creature's original (and sometimes very different) design appearing on the front. The Rancor, in particular, went through a number of significant changes before Lucas and company were satisfied with the savage monster's appearance.

Our third sub-set, "The Art of Star Wars," would showcase art that was designed for posters,

Luke Skywalker	Star Wars	Empire	Jedi
Knowledge			
Strength			
Mechanical Skill			
Weapons Ability			
Force Power			

Luke Skywalker	1	2	3	4	5	6	7	8	9	10
Knowledge										
Strength										
Mechanical Skill										
Weapons Ability										
Force Power										

illustrations that were generated by various manufacturers lucky enough to have obtained a product license, and art that was commissioned by Lucasfilm but not used for one reason or another.

Last and certainly not least, was the most elaborate and time-consuming of the GALAXY categories: "New Visions."

The concept was an art collector's dream come true... Top comic book/fantasy illustrators would be rendering their favorite characters, inventing situations that appealed to them, or depicting scenes that they always wanted to see. "This was our contribution to the art history of *Star Wars*," observes Topps Creative Director Len Brown. Equally entertaining, the card backs would offer engaging self-portraits (or photos) along with mini-bios of the various illustrators.

With the new, fully-developed outline okayed and a small

army of artists ready to tackle their respective visions, Sean Taggart was hired to coordinate and fine tune incoming art. In addition to trafficking this multi-faceted project through the Topps system, Sean became the stern-yet-sensitive voice on the other end of the line when artists were late with their artwork. Also engaged during this period was card designer Arnie Sawyer, who, working with Topps Art Director Brad Kahlhamer, absorbed our series-within-a-series format and developed some original layout and coloring schemes.

After a number of false starts and curious mutations, STAR WARS GALAXY was actually coming to life. Even so, an enormous amount of work remained to be done.

Photos had to be selected from Lucasfilm, along with whatever pre-existing art we intended to publish (which was considerable). Fronts and backs had to be

coordinated thematically. Chase cards had to be designed. Text chores - 140 card backs - were eventually divided between myself and Steve Sansweet.

STAR WARS GALAXY wound up being one of the most exhausting, yet most satisfying card sets we've ever produced. This companion book, the first of its kind from Topps, is intended not only as a portfolio of magnificent "New Visions" art, but as a tour through the unique process of developing such a collection for the trading card medium.

As George Lucas points out in our foreword, the creative journey is just beginning.

—*Gary Gerani*
1993

PRINCESS LEIA

J O E S M I T H

Artistically speaking, this is a tale of two Joes: Jusko, the MARVEL MASTERPIECES painter who was originally commissioned to render our "Ensemble" cards; and Smith, the acclaimed movie poster illustrator who ultimately did the job.

The "Ensemble" itself has its origins in one of our earlier outlines. We started out with about thirty subjects, including several second and third string characters. This was later cut down to the twelve most important heroes and villains.

I had introduced Joe Jusko to the world of trading card illustration with our TOXIC CRUSADERS series in 1991, and was looking forward to working with him on the more ambitious STAR WARS job. It wasn't meant to be: After providing us with a group of pencil roughs, Joe found himself overcommitted in other areas and bowed out of the assignment.

Enter Mr. Smith, the second of my artistic Joes.

"When Gary came over to visit, I had no idea I'd soon be painting a dozen portraits for Topps," laughs the 81-year old movie illustrator. "I came out of retirement to do the job and really had a grand time. Only Boba Fett gave me some grief. I did him twice. The first pass looked more like the toy figure of Boba than the real character."

Joe Smith's movie-related credits span close to six decades. He worked for Disney, Universal, MGM — all the major studios during their heyday. Charlton Heston remains his favorite actor subject, and the *Ben-Hur* poster (1959) with its famous "chiseled in stone" logo is arguably his finest achievement. Other notable campaigns include *Dr. Zhivago, Green Mansions, King of Kings, The Wonderful World of the Brothers Grimm* and sci-fi/horror classics such as *The Birds, Horror of Dracula, Gorgo* and *The Day of the Triffids.* ✳

C - 3 P O

YODA

LUKE SKYWALKER

CHEWBACCA

HAN SOLO

OBI-WAN KENOBI

DARTH VADER

THE EMPEROR

BOBA FETT

LANDO CALRISSIAN

R2-D2

When is a Wookiee not a Wookiee?

When it looks like an enraged abominable snowman, or maybe a werewolf on steroids. Such determinations were commonplace as George Lucas guided the development of his other-worldly entities. Fortunately, he had cinema's most gifted designers on his team: Ralph McQuarrie, whose evocative storyboard paintings helped sell the property in the first place; creature creators

Stuart Freeborn, Phil Tippett, Ron Cobb and Joe Johnston; costume designers Aggie Guerard Rodgers and Nilo Rodis-Jamero, and many, many others.

Everything in *Star Wars* had to be fabricated, since the galaxy in which the story takes place was not our galaxy — we learned that in the opening crawl. Yet there were similarities: the regal and political institutions, the World War II-like flavor of aerial combat, the existence of spiritual as well as scientific reality for the culture-at-large. George Lucas reasoned, quite shrewdly, that if viewers were asked to visit a cosmos so totally alien to their sensibilities, they'd have a hard time relating to the characters and enjoying the story. Unlike his own *THX 1138*, *Star Wars* was structured like a classic American western, or a fanciful reworking of the King

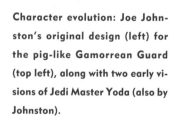

Character evolution: Joe Johnston's original design (left) for the pig-like Gamorrean Guard (top left), along with two early visions of Jedi Master Yoda (also by Johnston).

The vicious Rancor went through numerous design changes. Left: a pair of concepts by Joe Johnston. Below: the beast as it appears in a Ralph McQuarrie painting.

Arthur legend with spaceships and rayguns. This approach made the futuristic overlay warmer, more romantic... though just as difficult to achieve. Every vehicle, every weapon, every exotic lifeform had to be created from scratch.

To gather the rarest and most interesting design concepts, Steve Sansweet and I spent several days at Lucas' Skywalker Ranch in Northern California.

"We were like a couple of kids in a candy store," recalls Sansweet, "the Raiders of the Lucasfilm Archives. We turned up some really obscure and beautiful pieces. And there are still a few flat files that we haven't invaded yet!" ✳

Johnston strikes again with his initial conception of the AT-AT (left), later transformed into the stop-motion animated Snow Walkers of *The Empire Strikes Back* (above).

P
R
O
M
O
T
I
O
N
S

The colorful history of *Star Wars* can be traced through the breathtaking artwork commissioned for its advertising. Just as the trilogy rejuvenated mythic storytelling and provided high adventure on a scale recalling Hollywood's more flamboyant days, these illustrations reflected a return to spectacular, classical art influences.

Never before had a film's subject lent itself so readily to creative promotion.

Most fantasy movies offer one central element to exploit; one *King Kong*, one *Robocop*, one *Creature from the Black Lagoon*. But from the very first frame of *Star Wars* until the last, enthralled viewers were plunged into a fanciful cosmos inhabited by aliens, robots, weird creatures, fantastic vehicles and weaponry, swashbuckling heroes, enigmatic villains and just about anything a robust imagination might provide.

For filmgoers seeking escapism, it was nirvana. For painters and illustrators responsible for promoting the property, it became both a challenge and a delight to compress the fabulous *Star Wars* experience into self-contained, iconographic renderings.

Not all of the important posters developed for *Star Wars* were movie posters. Before the film was even finished the concept was being tested at science fiction and comic book conventions. The first memorable *Star Wars* poster was an early collage by comics artist Howard Chaykin. At the time this $1 poster was largely ignored — who ever heard of a space epic called *Star Wars*? Today, not surprisingly, it's a cherished collector's item worth over $400.

Since *Star Wars* quickly became a merchandising bonanza, companies with a license began developing their own wonderful posters and promotional illustrations. An excellent example is the series of paintings by celebrated fantasy illustrator Boris Vallejo, depicting scenes from *The Empire Strikes Back* for a

Coca-Cola tie-in campaign. Other striking creations include the commemorative plate collection by Thomas Blackshear, Drew Struzan's Young Adult novel covers, and Dave Dorman's paintings for the new Dark Horse comic book series.

Of course, the beauty and impact of the actual movie posters shouldn't be minimized. The original Tom Jung one-sheet art quickly became as emblematic of *Star Wars* as John Williams'

Three striking posters from three remarkable artists: Drew Struzan (far left), noted movie poster illustrator; Howard Chaykin (left) from the comics field; and Japanese painter Noriyoshi Ohrai (above).

rousing musical score. Roger Kastel's key painting for *The Empire Strikes Back*, which featured Han and Leia in an epic romantic embrace, was a canny homage to the famous *Gone With The Wind* poster design. And across the world, artists from various countries and cultures lent their own imaginations to the inspiring task of promoting George Lucas' blockbuster trilogy. ✳

Darth Vader: three illustrations dominated by the Dark Lord of the Sith. Left: an unused pencil rendering for *The Empire Strikes Back* by Sanjulian. Upper right: Witold Dybowski's *Return of the Jedi* poster (Poland). Lower right: Coca-Cola tie-in campaign by Boris Vallejo.

Colorist: Arthur Suydam

THE CHASE CARDS

Chase cards have become an integral part of collectible trading card products in recent years. Randomly inserted into card packs, they are generally printed in some exotic fashion to distinguish them from the main set. The six character chase cards for STAR WARS GALAXY employed etched foil technology to create a lustrous, textured effect.

After completing his "New Visions" illustration, Walter Simonson was commissioned to depict an exciting potpourri of *Star Wars* events. Each of the foil cards was designed to function as a self-contained character illustration; put all six together and they form one exciting, epic rendering. (For more information on Walter Simonson, please turn to page 100.)

"Collectors told us they loved the cards" offers Greg Goldstein, Topps Director of Publishing Operations. "But we know we can improve the technology and make them even more exciting the next time" ✳

NEWVISIONS ▶

KYLE BAKER

"The injured Chewie is reaching over the rail for the dangling Han, who is, in turn, blindly reaching down toward the desperate Lando. One of the Sarlacc's tentacles has wrapped tightly around Lando's ankle, dragging him down the side of the pit.."

from the "Return of the Jedi" screenplay

"*Star Wars* was one of my favorite movies as a child," recalls Kyle Baker, "so it was a joy working on this project. It was also a bit of a challenge. By the time I got around to doing my card, all of the scenes that I was thinking about doing were taken by other artists, and I ended up with The Evil Hole-In-The-Ground. I chose to show it from this odd perspective because nobody at Topps or Lucasfilm was able to provide me with the appropriate reference material!"

Baker started drawing comics for Marvel and DC back in 1984, and has also written and drawn two graphic novels, WHY I HATE SATURN and THE COWBOY WALLY SHOW. His work has appeared in SPY, THE VILLAGE VOICE, ESQUIRE, NATIONAL LAMPOON and other publications too numerous and low-paying to mention. Currently, Baker has a regular page in VIBE magazine. ✳

Held upside-down by Chewbacca, the still-blind Han Solo (Harrison Ford) strives valiantly to rescue his friend Lando Calrissian (Billy Dee Williams) from the monstrous maw of the Sarlacc. This exciting scene from *Return of the Jedi* was filmed in Yuma, Arizona, in a location known as Buttercup Valley. Since many of Jabba's evil cohorts wind up tumbling into the Sarlacc's huge "mouth," the monster was constructed with special equipment rigged to break the falls of the stuntmen.

Kyle Baker rented *Return of the Jedi* from his local video store and rendered his piece while watching the TV screen. "I never got a real good look at anything," the artist admits, "so I figured I'd better play it safe with a bizarre perspective." This classic case of necessity being the mother of invention resulted in a striking and stylish painting, an ideal choice to begin the "New Visions" portion of STAR WARS GALAXY. Baker used a black pencil and oil paint to bring his creation to life.

B
R
E
T
B
L
E
V
I
N
S

"Leia, dressed in the skimpy costume of a dancing girl, emerges onto the deck as Luke turns to face another guard. She turns to the barge cannon, climbs on the platform, and swivels the gun around..."

from the "Return of the Jedi" screenplay

"The character of Princess Leia combines the qualities of charm, whimsy, nobility, and just plain fun that defines *Star Wars* for me," offers Bret Blevins. "And besides, I love this costume."

Illustrator Blevins is a long time fan of fabled fantasy. "My main interest in visualizing an idea," he explains, "is composing the design of an image — arranging the elements of a complicated scene for absolute clarity, without losing a feeling of naturalness and spontaneity. I never tire of this particular challenge and would have to say that it's the main attraction of picture-making for me."

Blevins began his career in the comics field with his 1982 adaptation of THE DARK CRYSTAL for Marvel. Since then he's rendered "buckets of stuff," including THE NEW MUTANTS, THE BOZZ CHRONICLES, BATMAN, TARZAN and THE TROUBLE WITH GIRLS. ✳

Princess Leia (Carrie Fisher) emerges on the deck of the prison barge and joins in the furious battle against Jabba's mercenaries. Fisher, the daughter of actress Debbie Reynolds and singer Eddie Fisher, was the youngest member of the original *Star Wars* cast. But "she was very worldly, very self-assured," George Lucas remembers. Fisher currently enjoys twin careers as a film actress and a popular novelist.

"My goal in the creation of the Princess Leia card was to strike a sort of cross between a Golden Age comic book cover and an old Saturday morning serial poster," says Bret Blevins. The artist generally uses soft graphite leads for pencil work — 2H and HB — filling large black areas with a 5H to reduce smudging. He favors Langnickel sable brushes and Gilliot 303 or Hunt 108 pen nibs for inking.

T E D   B O O N T H A N A K I T

"Leia turns from the spectacle outside, leaps onto Jabba's throne, and throws the chain that enslaves her over his head around his bulbous neck. Then she dives off the other side of the throne, pulling the chain violently in her grasp..."

from the "Return of the Jedi" screenplay

A sleek, sexy, almost Amazonian Princess Leia is Jabba's prize catch and worst nightmare. "Lying on the ground during a safari," recalls Ted Boonthanakit, "I'd look up at the sky and wonder: are there really Darth Vaders up there?"

Born in Bangkok, Thailand, Boonthanakit spent his formative years in Kenya. Like an infinite number of artists before him, the young illustrator was inspired to immortalize African wildlife. Then, in the mid-'70s, Boonthanakit stumbled upon a newsstand, discovered Marvel and DC Comics...and the course of his creative career changed dramatically.

Now based in Atlanta, Georgia, he divides his time between comics (MICRA, written by Lamar Waldron), advertising, movie storyboarding (Renny Harlin's *Cutthroat Island*, Michael Jackson music videos and *Addams Family II*), and Topps trading card illustrations. ✳

Her attempt to rescue Han Solo thwarted, Princess Leia (Carrie Fisher) is captured by Jabba and dressed in a skimpy dancing girl outfit. "(Jabba) is what he is," the actress quips. "He doesn't pretend to be anything else. He doesn't feel the need to be charming. He's just an unpretentious, straightforward kind of guy..."

Jabba the Hutt became more of a metaphysical background element as Ted Boonthanakit's pencil design progressed. This suggests that the gangster slug is clearly on the mind of our knife-wielding, extremely angry, warrior-like Princess Leia. Amazingly, the colorful finish was accomplished almost entirely with markers, with a few highlights achieved by Prisma colored pencils.

J U N E · B R I G M A N

"Leia races for the remaining speeder bike. The two fleeing Imperial scouts have a good lead as Luke and Leia pursue through the giant trees at 200 miles an hour. Leia guns it, closing the gap, as the two scouts recklessly veer through a narrow gap in the trees…"

from the "Return of the Jedi" screenplay

"All three *Star Wars* films have great joy-ride scenes," remembers June Brigman. "The speeder bike chase from *Return of the Jedi* is one of my favorites."

Brigman began working as an artist for Marvel Comics at age 22. Although continually active in the comics field, she also works in advertising and produces a monthly comic strip for NATIONAL GEOGRAPHIC WORLD magazine. Brigman recently illus-

trated three STAR WARS Young Adult novels, three "Choose Your Own Adventure" books (both for Bantam Doubleday Dell) and did new line art for Ballantine's book A GUIDE TO THE STAR WARS UNIVERSE, Second Edition. Other projects include the WHERE IN THE WORLD IS CARMEN SANDIEGO? comic strip for NATIONAL GEOGRAPHIC WORLD and a four-issue SUPERGIRL mini-series for DC Comics. ✳

Setting: the forested moon of Endor. Recovering from the speeder bike chase, Princess Leia (Carrie Fisher) meets up with an inquisitive little Ewok (Warwick Davis) and the two become fast friends. Originally, George Lucas planned to have the Imperial forces overthrown by the primitive rage of the Wookiees in a thrilling land-and-space battle. When Chewbacca became established as a relatively sophisticated character, this idea was abandoned and the Ewoks were born.

June Brigman rendered her STAR WARS GALAXY illustration with "pen, black ink and a good deal of nostalgia." The artist has tremendous admiration for George Lucas' ground-breaking trilogy. "What impresses me most about the *Star Wars* phenomenon is its longevity," she comments. "Years after *Star Wars* first hit the screen, the movies and the spin-off merchandising con-tinue to have a huge following. Some of the biggest *Star Wars* fans weren't even born when the first movie was released. I think it's neat that my grandchildren could be *Star Wars* fans."

ADVENTURE ON THE HORIZON

"The giant twin suns of Tatooine slowly disappear behind a distant dune range. Luke stands watching them for a few moments, then reluctantly enters the domed entrance to the homestead..."

from the "Star Wars" screenplay

After his uncle forbids him to apply to the Academy, Luke stares at the sunset, yearning for adventure. "It's a favorite moment of mine," reflects Paul Chadwick, "unusually quiet but full of wonder. The way the twin suns are revealed without comment or emphasis is delicious, as we appreciate that their weird beauty is commonplace to him."

Chadwick began his career painting SF book covers and drawing movie storyboards, but eventually turned to comics in 1984, penciling Marvel's DAZZLER. By 1986 his own creation CONCRETE began appearing in Dark Horse comics, and it continues in various incarnations to this day. In 1994 a CONCRETE mini-series "Killer Smile" will appear under the dual Dark Horse and Legend imprints.

With Larry Wilson, Chadwick has completed a screenplay for a movie version of CONCRETE, and they are currently working on a screenplay based on Thomas Easton's ORGANIC FUTURE stories. ✳

Somewhere beyond Tatooine's twin suns, or at least over the rainbow, an exciting destiny awaits restless farmboy Luke Skywalker (Mark Hamill). "Luke is very simple, very naive, very straightforward," says Hamill. "He's that classic character in literature that doesn't want to stay on the farm, that wants to see what's beyond..."

"This artwork was executed in the manner of the master movie poster artist, Drew Struzan," explains Paul Chadwick. "After the usual preliminary work, a detailed drawing is done on the board with colored pencil. The acrylic paint is airbrushed without frisket, letting colors blend into each other, letting the pencil lines hold the form. Light modeling is done with colored pencil and a few highlights of white acrylic paint are then added."

CHADWICK

H O W A R D C H A Y K I N

"Luke climbs up into the cockpit of his fighter and puts on his helmet. Threepio looks on from the floor of the massive hangar as the crewmen secure his little electronic partner into Luke's X-wing. It's an emotion-filled moment as Artoo-Detoo beeps goodbye…"

from the "Star Wars" screenplay

"**M**y favorite sequence in *Star Wars* is the assault on the Death Star," says Howard Chaykin, "with its references to all those terrific air war pictures of the late '40s to the mid-'50s. *Star Wars* remains a pivotal pop cultural event for me. Now if it had only been around when I was seventeen — and still possessed a genuine sense of wonder…"

Chaykin pioneered the graphic novel form with EMPIRE and THE STARS MY DESTINATION, deconstructed a number of mainstream characters in the '80s (most notably THE SHADOW and BLACKHAWK), created AMERICAN FLAGG!, TIME[2] and BLACK KISS, recently wrote and drew MIDNIGHT MEN for Epic, and is writing and drawing POWER & GLORY for Bravura. ✳

The climax of *Star Wars*: Pilot Luke Skywalker (Mark Hamill) boards his X-wing as the Rebels prepare for their fateful raid on the Death Star battle station. Hamill, 25 when he made the film, was and remains a tremendous fan of fantasy and science fiction. He currently provides the voice of the Joker in Fox's Emmy-winning *Batman: The Animated Series*.

"After years of dumping on technique, I now stand in awe of the great technicians of comics," admits Howard Chaykin. "Not being one of those, I'm forced by my own abilities to make assets out of limitations — and to achieve maximum effects with the simplest line style possible. My idol and role model is clearly Alex Toth, a legend among discerning artists, if not of the average fanboy."

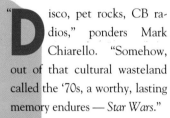

MARK CHIARELLO

"A shabby old desert-rat-of-a-man appears and leans over Luke. His ancient leathery face, cracked and weathered by exotic climates is set off by dark, penetrating eyes and a scraggly white beard. Ben Kenobi squints his eyes as he scrutinizes the unconscious farmboy…"

from the "Star Wars" screenplay

"**D**isco, pet rocks, CB radios," ponders Mark Chiarello. "Somehow, out of that cultural wasteland called the '70s, a worthy, lasting memory endures — *Star Wars*."

Chiarello considers George Lucas' original film something of a daring experiment. "The fact that Alec Guinness was in the movie lent some credibility (to the project). Here's this phenomenal actor, probably the greatest actor of all time as far as I'm concerned, in the middle of this really hip surfing movie!"

Reflecting the Alec Guinness stability factor, Chiarello deliberately avoided airbrushed laser effects and other flashy gimmicks. "I did a serious portrait of a serious actor," he says with pride.

Chiarello's comics-related work includes the STARS OF THE NEGRO LEAGUE card set, short stories for THE RAY BRADBURY CHRONICLES and HELLRAISER, coloring and portrait work for BRAM STOKER'S DRACULA (Topps) and the Batman/Houdini graphic novel, THE DEVIL'S WORKSHOP, published by DC Comics.

His upcoming projects are decidedly horrific: a new comics version of *The Night Stalker* for Topps, and a series of scenes from the original 1931 Frankenstein for the Topps UNIVERSAL MONSTERS card set. ✱

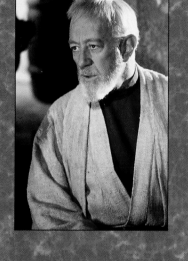

"My role in *Star Wars* has been described as a blend of the wizard Merlin and a Samurai warrior," reflects Alec Guinness with a grin, "and you can't beat that!" One of cinema's most acclaimed actors, Guinness won an Oscar for his performance in *The Bridge on the River Kwai* and has appeared in several other David Lean films, including *Great Expectations* and *Lawrence of Arabia* . "When I read the script for *Star Wars*," he remembers, "it had something that made me high, held my attention. It was an adventure story about the passing of knowledge and the sword from one generation to the next…"

Unlike most of the artists who contributed to STAR WARS GALAXY, Mark Chiarello did not provide a preliminary pencil design. "Since the Obi-Wan piece was going to be a portrait there really wasn't any reason to," the artist explains.

Chiarello uses water colors exclusively. His distinctive creations come to life "a little bit like a jigsaw puzzle," he points out, "with one small colored shape connecting to another, then another, and so on. Finally, all of these connected or overlapped visual elements come together to form the finished portrait."

CHIARELLO

G E O F D A R R O W

"A weird mechanical sound rises above the whining of the wind. A strange probe robot, with several extended sensors, emerges from the smoke-shrouded crater. The ominous mechanical probe floats across the snow plain and disappears into the distance…"

from "The Empire Strikes Back" screenplay

Geof Darrow "saw *Star Wars* 18 different times in the theater, not on video, like most weenies in America today. It's still my No. 1 favorite movie. Illustrating the Probots was a great way to pay homage to George Lucas and the science fiction comics (especially the work of Jean 'Moebius' Giraud) that inspired him. Thanks George!"

After working as a cartoonist for Filmation and Hanna-Barbera, Darrow moved to Paris, France where he collaborated with Moebius on the CITY OF FIRE portfolio. Then it was back to Los Angeles where he and Frank Miller developed HARD BOILED and eventually BIG GUY AND RUSTY THE BOY ROBOT. Darrow's currently working on an original BIG GUY story for Legend/Dark Horse Comics, "where Tokyo is overrun by monsters." ✳

Chewbacca (Peter Mayhew) plays a deadly game of hide-and-seek with the Imperial Probe Droid, or "Probot," dispatched by the Empire to track down and obliterate the Rebels. Originally, the Probot performed more on-screen mayhem, and a panel reflecting this actually turned up in the Archie Goodwin/Al Williamson comics adaptation of *The Empire Strikes Back.*

Penciler/inker Geof Darrow experimented with Luke's landspeeder before settling on the "Probot attack" for his GALAXY piece. Reveals the artist: "I found in illustrating *Star Wars* scenes that I achieved the best result while wearing navy blue, size 13 Converse All Stars. The extra traction they gave really came in handy on the curves in the Probot's external armor."

S T E V E D I T K O

"Eight Jawas carry Artoo out of the canyon to a huge tank-like vehicle the size of a four-story house. The filthy little Jawas scurry like rats up small ladders and enter the main cabin of the behemoth transport…"

from the "Star Wars" screenplay

"I don't understand how that is meant," answers Steve Ditko when asked about what inspired him to do this *Star Wars* rendering. "The card situation was given to me to illustrate."

Ditko is one of the most respected names in the comic book cosmos, having pioneered the visual styles of classic Marvel characters like THE AMAZING SPIDER-MAN and DR. STRANGE, as well as creating ground-breaking characters of his own, such as the critically-acclaimed MR. A. Other fine work appears in Warren horror comics of the '60s and various "monster movie" series (GORGO, KONGA, etc.) published by Charlton during the same period.

Recently, he rendered JACK KIRBY'S SECRET CITY SAGA for Topps Comics. ✳

Steve Ditko's unusual take on the Sandcrawler sequence from *Star Wars* was frequently mistaken for a horizontal image. To help clarify things, foreground elements (including a droid wearing a shoe) were added after the original inked piece was completed.

On Tatooine, R2-D2 (Kenny Baker) is captured by the ratlike Jawas and imprisoned within the huge metal walls of their Sandcrawler. Explains producer Gary Kurtz: "The long shots of the Sandcrawler are a miniature - for the shots of it rolling across the desert. We did film a full-sized piece of it that was about 40 feet high and 125 feet long. We investigated the possibility of using a real, very large earth mover or some such vehicle - but they were not where we needed them and were also very expenisve to rent. We found it was better to do it on our own."

DAVE DORMAN

"Artoo enters a wide room with a four-foot ceiling. In the middle of the scrap heap sit a dozen or so robots of various shapes and sizes. Some are engaged in electronic conversation, while others simply mill about..."

from the "Star Wars" screenplay

"**A**lthough they may play a minor role, the droids are the indispensable workhorses of the *Star Wars* movie universe, and deserve to be spotlighted," observes Dave Dorman. "Just recently, over the last four or five years, I've been leaning more toward mechanical elements in my artwork. With the droids, not only am I painting nuts and bolts, but these characters actually represent nuts and bolts."

An illustrator for twelve years, Dorman is best known for his photo-realistic rendering of adventure and science fiction subjects, including BATMAN, STAR WARS, INDIANA JONES, and DUNGEONS AND DRAGONS. ALIENS: TRIBES, an illustrated novel featuring 24 of his paintings, has recently been released.

Turning from contemporary science fiction greats to the classics, Dorman painted sequential scenes from 1957's *The Incredible Shrinking Man* for Topps' new UNIVERSAL MONSTERS card set. "From George Lucas' droids to Robert Scott Carey fighting a spider," the artist reflects, "it's been an interesting period." ✳

Droid sale: Robots captured by the Jawas on Tatooine are peddled to local farmers, including Luke's Uncle Owen. 25 different droid model styles were developed for this sequence, which was filmed in the Tunisian desert. "The trouble with the future in most futuristic movies is that it always looks new and clean and shiny," observes George Lucas. "What is required for true credibility is a used future..."

After Dave Dorman's pencil rough was approved, he embarked on his finish utilizing both oil paint and acrylics. Dorman achieves stunning results treating oil like water color, texturing his backgrounds and laying acrylic detail on top of that.

A DEAL GETTING WORSE ALL THE TIME

"Four armor-suited stormtroopers stand at the ready in the large carbon-freezing chamber, which is filled with pipes and chemical tanks. In the middle of the room is a round pit housing a hydraulic platform. Darth Vader and Lando stand near the platform. Lando's face registers dismay..."

from "The Empire Strikes Back" screenplay

George Evans on George Lucas: "It's said that he was inspired to do a tribute to the beautiful old FLASH GORDON Sunday comic as a long time fan. He took this George along on one wonderful time machine trip with him!"

Known for his classic plane and aerial renderings, veteran illustrator Evans worked on pulp mags and comics during the '40s after his Air Force service in World War II. Among the influential companies he's worked for are Fiction House, Fawcett and E.C. under Bill Gaines. Evans currently renders the SECRET AGENT CORRIGAN strip for King Features.

"When I watched the various *Star Wars* movies and saw the various books my grandchildren had on *Star Wars*," the artist remembers, "I didn't recall seeing much of anything between Lando and the Princess. For me, human interplay, human interest is the soul of an illustration. Even my aerial work...I always try to do the plane so that somebody — the viewer — is 'in' the picture." ✳

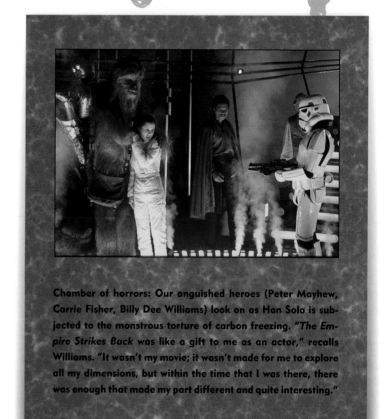

Chamber of horrors: Our anguished heroes (Peter Mayhew, Carrie Fisher, Billy Dee Williams) look on as Han Solo is subjected to the monstrous torture of carbon freezing. *"The Empire Strikes Back* was like a gift to me as an actor," recalls Williams. "It wasn't my movie; it wasn't made for me to explore all my dimensions, but within the time that I was there, there was enough that made my part different and quite interesting."

George Evans' original pencil rough offered Lando in a more exaggerated perspective. For the finish, Evans used mixed media: acrylic paint, with colored pencils for fine details. This enabled the artist to match every color perfectly, and also created a "glowing" effect.

F
A
S
T
N
E
R
&
L
A
R
S
O
N

"Suddenly the walls of the garbage receptacle shudder and move in a couple of inches. Han and Leia place poles and long metal beams between the closing walls, but they are simply snapped and bent as the giant trashmasher rumbles on…"

from the "Star Wars" screenplay

Say Steve Fastner and Rich Larson: "We always thought that Leia Organa — smarter, wittier, and yes, manlier than her cohorts — should've been the one to slay the garbage chute eyeball monster. Luke, after all, is a farm boy, and Han's a cynical mercenary. But Leia's a Royal in the best sense: she assumes responsibility, exudes authority and commands respect. Her cause is important and just."

Seriously wacked out on early Marvels, psychotronic movies and good girl art, Fastner and Larson have produced lurid airbrush fantasies for comics, paperbacks and records since 1976. Their trend-setting BARBARIAN BABE portfolios are available from S.Q.P. *

Aboard the Death Star, our four adventurers (Mark Hamill, Harrison Ford, Carrie Fisher and Peter Mayhew) are about to be flattened by the inexorable assault of the garbage crusher. The familiar "walls are moving!" routine was a standard in movie melodramas and serials of the '30s and '40s. Certainly, FLASH GORDON, JOHN CARTER OF MARS and Edwin Arnold's 1905 tale GULLIVER ON MARS were significant *Star Wars* influences.

Steve Fastner and Rich Larson worked in some amusing SF icons while tackling their pencil rough (Robby the Robot was in the trash on the left); these were removed for the finished painting. Fastner uses marker and airbrush directly over a xerox of Larson's pencils, in a technique he says he devised and perfected himself, but in actuality probably stole from the Russians.

K E I T H G I F F E N

"Walking toward them out of the darkness is Bib Fortuna, a humanlike alien with long tentacles protruding from his skull. Bib holds out his hand toward Artoo and the tiny droid backs up a bit, letting out a protesting array of squeaks. Threepio turns to the strange-looking alien…"

from the "Return of the Jedi" screenplay

Noted comics illustrator Keith Giffen stands by an unsubstantiated claim that he was reincarnated from Bantha stock. His choice of character was motivated by an intense fascination with anybody named after an infant drool catcher. Indeed, Jabba's right-hand entity, Bib Fortuna, never looked so intriguing. "I was tow-headed myself as a youth," the artist admits. "It's no wonder that Bib Fortuna continues to fascinate me."

Giffen's memorable work includes the retooling of JUSTICE LEAGUE OF AMERICA and LEGION OF SUPERHEROES for DC and his tough-as-nails creations LOBO and TRENCHER, the latter under the newly-formed Black Ball imprint. He's also plotting the new FREAK FORCE book for Erik Larsen. ✳

Jabba's gruesome right-hand creature, Bib Fortuna (Michael Carter), has a devilish glint in his alien eyes. Bib was one of the strangest entities appearing in *Return of the Jedi* (which is saying a lot). In some ways, he resembles the legendary vampire Nosferatu - evil yet elegant, with distorted extremities.

Keith Giffen explains how he does it: "It's that Bantha work ethic. You know, eight hours a day, five days a week. Sure it's radical, but that's just the kind of guy I am. I also prefer working directly in ink using various rapidograph pen point sizes. It forces a spontaneity that I've never been able to achieve with a 'pencil first' approach."

P
A
U
L
G
U
L
A
C
Y

"Luke finishes off the last guard on the second skiff. He sees the deck gun blasting away at his helpless companions. Luke leaps from the skiff, across a chasm of air, to the sheer metallic side of the Sail Barge…"

from the "Return of the Jedi" screenplay

"*Star Wars* to me was the perfect fusion of science fiction, fairy tale, comic book and cinematic escapism," asserts Paul Gulacy. If (this illustration) is as close as I can get to being associated with the *Star Wars* phenomenon, I'll take it. I'm looking forward to the next trilogy…Thank you, Mr. Lucas and company!"

Gulacy first achieved fame with Marvel's MASTER OF KUNG FU ('74 - '77), then continued

to dazzle comics fans with SABRE, NIGHTMARES, SIX FROM SIRUS, BATMAN (in '86), CO- NAN, VALKYRIE! and JAMES BOND and THE TERMINATOR for Dark Horse. Upcoming projects include THE THING FROM AN- OTHER WORLD (Dark Horse), a new BATMAN VS. PREDATOR (DC/Dark Horse) and BATMAN: ELSEWORLD, from DC. ✳

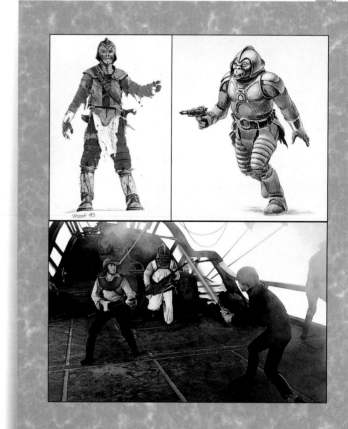

Klaatu was one of several alien mercenaries throttled by Luke in *Return of the Jedi*'s prison barge battle. His name was de- rived from the famous character portrayed by Michael Rennie in the science fiction classic *The Day the Earth Stood Still*. These two concept designs reflect early interpretations of Klaatu and one of Jabba's piglike Gamorrean Guards.

"I had a ball drawing the two mercenaries (from *Return of the Jedi*), but Id've much preferred Habba the Jut," quips Paul Gulacy. Most of the artist's cre- ations have been rendered in oil and acrylic, but his favorite paint is cel vinyl, a paint used mainly by animators. Gulacy's GALAXY piece was done in cel vinyl, markers and watercolor.

BO HAMPTON

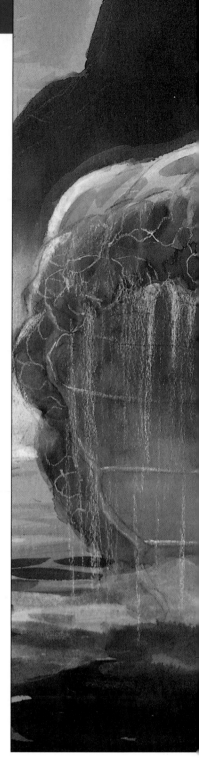

CONFRONTATION ON DAGOBAH

"The young Jedi surveys the fog, which is barely pierced by the ship's landing lights. About all he can detect are some giant, twisted trees nearby. Artoo whistles anxiously..."

"The mist has dispersed a bit, but it is still a very gloomy-looking swamp..."

from "The Empire Strikes Back" screenplay

"I wanted to do Han Solo on Dagobah mainly because I like the character and I like the planet," explains Bo Hampton. "Where else but in science fiction can you make a statement like that?"

After assisting his former teacher, Wil Eisner, back in the late '70s, Hampton broke into the comics biz with limited work for DC's WITCHING HOUR. He was also involved in the original *Star Wars* newspaper strip, inking a few machines and robots for Al Williamson. Recent projects in-clude LEGEND OF SLEEPY HOLLOW for Tundra and UTHER, THE HALF-DEAD KING for Tundra, U.K.

"I really enjoyed working on my GALAXY trading card that featured Han and Boba Fett," Hampton concludes. "Gary Gerani asked me who would have prevailed in that contest, and it seems to me from the de-meanor of the creature (Fett is riding) that it very likely would have eaten them both. But not eaten as in dead...eaten as in cliffhanger!" ✳

Luke (Mark Hamill) can't believe his eyes when Jedi Master Yoda uses the Force to levitate his downed X-wing out of a swamp. Planet Dagobah was a memorable "location," creat-ed and contained on an extra-large sound stage at Elstree Stu-dios in England. The X-wing used in this sequence was both a full-size prop and an Industrial Light and Magic miniature.

Bo Hampton worked larger than most of the other GALAXY artists — his piece measured 13" x 18". The matte board he used was greenish-gray in color, and it is this hue that winds up dominating the finished painting. He used gouache and watercolor over his pencil work.

S
C
O
T
T
H
A
M
P
T
O
N

"Suddenly all heads turn as Commander Tagge's speech is cut short and the Grand Moff Tarkin, governor of the Imperial outland regions, enters. All of the generals stand and bow before the thin, evil-looking governor as he takes his place at the head of the table…"

from the "Star Wars" screenplay

Striking a pleasant smile, Grand Moff Tarkin clearly fancies himself "a good man"…in spite of the fact that he blows away planets and enslaves half the galaxy.

"I've been a Peter Cushing fan since those halcyon days of Hammer," offers Scott Hampton. "It was a pleasure painting one of the great faces of film. As far as I'm concerned, both Cushing and Alex Guinness added a touch of class to the *Star Wars* trilogy, and made the films really sing."

Hampton began his illustration career in 1983, rendering SILVERHEELS for Pacific Comics. Marvel's EPIC ILLUSTRATED followed, along with HELLRAISER and various graphic novels including BOOKS OF MAGIC, BATMAN: NIGHTCRIES, and one of his finest offerings, an adaptation of Robert E. Howard's PIGEONS FROM HELL. Recently Hampton wrote and illustrated "The Sleeping" for DC's LEGENDS OF THE DARK KNIGHT, and a graphic novel entitled THE UP-TURNED STONE. ✳

The sinister Grand Moff Tarkin was a plum role for veteran fantasy film star Peter Cushing. Along with Alec Guinness, Cushing registers as the face of sophisticated adulthood in a universe populated mostly by teenagers or twentysomethings. The British performer is perhaps best known for his appearances in "Hammer" horror movies, in which he was frequently paired with Christopher Lee. Cushing also had roles in several film classics, including Laurence Olivier's *Hamlet* and John Huston's *Moulin Rouge*.

Scott Hampton always envisioned Grand Moff Tarkin in profile, although the Imperial bigwig's nasty little smile wasn't quite so pronounced in the original pencil rough. For his finish, Hampton used mixed media: Windsor & Newton water colors, selected inks, acrylics, thinned oils and colored pencils.

M I C H A E L W M. K A L U T A

"Conferring with Mon Mothma are several military leaders, including General Madine and Admiral Ackbar (a salmon-colored Mon Calamari). Ackbar steps forward, pointing to a holographic model of the Death Star, the Endor moon and the protecting deflector shield in the center of the room…"

from the "Return of the Jedi" screenplay

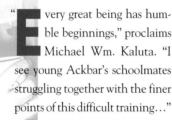

"Every great being has humble beginnings," proclaims Michael Wm. Kaluta. "I see young Ackbar's schoolmates struggling together with the finer points of this difficult training…"

In 1969 the prolific Kaluta began working for DC Comics. Jobs on BATMAN, DETECTIVE and one of his most critically-acclaimed assignments, THE SHADOW, followed. Other well-known works include STARSTRUCK (for Marvel/Epic), MY NAME IS PARIS, BILL THE GALACTIC HERO and THE ABYSS.

Currently, Kaluta has contributed to the 1994 TOLKIEN CALENDAR from Ballantine, THE GALACTIC GIRL GUIDES (a spin-off of STARSTRUCK, from Kitchen Sink), the four-issue PRINCE VALIANT comic from Marvel (covers); and will have his work showcased in a set of art cards from the Friedlander Publishing Group. ✳

"Once I figured on backtracking to a period before the movies," explains Michael Wm. Kaluta, "everything became easier. Satisfied with the composition and drawing elements of my pencil design, I traced the rendering onto Strathmore 3-ply kid finish paper. After the tracing, done with a Mongul #3 pencil, was

Admiral Ackbar (Tim Rose), member of a species known as Mon Calimari, prepares to take on the evil Empire at the climax of *Return of the Jedi*. The Winston Churchill-like commander was once described by actor Billy Dee Williams as a combination Lobster Man/Creature from the Black Lagoon. There were actually two versions of the admirable admiral: one for long shots, and a more detailed, fully-articulated incarnation for close-ups.

done, I erased it, using a kneaded eraser, which leaves the ghost of the image on the paper. I then drew over this ghost image, refining a final time. Once the drawing was finalized in pencil, I inked the entire picture, then began the water color process. The grid in the background was left unsprayed so it would bleed out, suggesting depth. I added a touch of white ink to the finished piece to pop some of the details out, and to add some life to the eyes of Ackbar and his schoolmates."

"Luke fires his laser pistol wildly as he and Leia rush down a narrow subhallway, chased by several stormtroopers..." "Before even thinking, Han draws his laser pistol and charges the troops, firing. His blast knocks one of the stormtroopers into the air..."

from the "Star Wars" screenplay

GIL KANE

"**I**'ve wanted to do STAR WARS for years," admits comics veteran Gil Kane. "I was most happy at the opportunity to add (George Lucas' creations) to a long list of characters I've done that go back, seemingly, to the beginning of time."

Kane's career in comics spans five decades. He began back in the 1940's with INSPECTOR BENTLEY OF SCOTLAND YARD for Pep Comics. This led to lucrative jobs for DC and eventually Marvel, as well as a fill-in stint on PRINCE VALIANT and long-term assignments on the TARZAN and STAR HAWKS newspaper strips. Over the years he's drawn just about every major character in the DC and Marvel Universes and recently finished his first assignment for Topps Comics, the official *Jurassic Park* adaptation .

Kane's most recent work is THE KILLING MACHINE for DC Comics, and he is currently working on EDGE for Bravura and a revival of his groundbreaking HIS NAME IS...SAVAGE. ✳

In the tradition of all swashbuckling space heroes, Luke (Mark Hamill) and Han (Harrison Ford) take aim at cosmic bad guys. "I think one of the key factors in the success of *Star Wars* is that it was a positive film, that it had heroes and villains, and that it was essentially a fun movie to watch," concludes creator George Lucas.

Han Solo appears to be defying the laws of physics in a pencil design that captures the outrageous-but-always-entertaining spirit of the *Star Wars* movies themselves. The artist works exclusively in pencil and ink.

C A M K E N N E D Y

"Darth Vader stands in the back control area of his ship's bridge with a motley group of men and creatures. Admiral Piett and two controllers stand at the front of the bridge and watch the group of bounty hunters with scorn…"

from "The Empire Strikes Back" screenplay

"**S**tar Wars has given me the chance to contribute to an already established and wonderful concept," observes Cam Kennedy. The ruthless bounty hunter Boba Fett (pictured here with an equally sinister colleague, Dengar) is one of his favorite characters.

Kennedy lives and works in Scotland. The illustrator of Dark Horse's STAR WARS: DARK EMPIRE (interiors), Kennedy has also scored big with OUTCASTS, SPECTRE, DAREDEVIL, BATMAN and LOBO, as well and JUDGE DREDD and ROGUE TROOPER for Europe.

✳

Darth Vader (David Prowse) checks out the rogue's gallery of galactic bounty hunters he's assembled in *The Empire Strikes Back*. Only one, Boba Fett (Jeremy Bulloch), will zero in on our heroes and win Jabba the Hutt's blood money for capturing Han Solo.

Cam Kennedy approached his STAR WARS GALAXY assignment by rendering the two figures first, capturing every detail and nuance. Later it was decided that subdued background elements (including the Millennium Falcon, on its way to the Cloud City of Bespin), would enable the illustration to "tell more of a story."

D A L E K E O W N

"A huge mechanical tong lifts the steaming metal-encased space pirate out of the vat and stands him on the platform. Some Ugnaughts rush over and push the block over onto the platform. They slide the coffinlike structure to the block…"

from "The Empire Strikes Back" screenplay

"*Star Wars* has had a huge impact on me," reveals Dale Keown. "At the time of its release, I strapped a small tape recorder to my stomach, and taped the audio portion of the movie so I could take it home and listen to it while I flipped through the STAR WARS comic book adaptation."

One of the most popular and critically-acclaimed artists in the comics biz, Keown's works include SAMURAI, DRAGON-RING, and DRAGON FORCE

(Aircel), Nth MAN and INCREDI-BLE HULK (Marvel) and one of his favorite projects ("I'll be do-ing this one for as long as I can…great fun!") entitled PITT, for Image Comics. ✳

Toward the end of *The Empire Strikes Back*, hero Han Solo (Harrison Ford) is carbon-frozen alive and taken away by boun-ty hunter Boba Fett. Solo's famous, final reply to his heartbro-ken princess (Leia: "I love you!" Han: "I know.") was improvised by actor Ford on the set. Some of Ford's other films include *American Grafitti*, *Witness*, *The Fugitive* and all three Indiana Jones adventures.

Dale Keown explains the evolu-tion of his GALAXY trading card illo: "When I received the call from Topps I was given a list of existing subjects to choose from. The Chewbacca card (my first choice) was already spoken for…DAMN! That's what you get for procrastinating, eh? Don't get me wrong — in retrospect, and seeing how Harrison Ford has become such a superstar — I think I made a good choice and I'm very happy with the end re-sult. As far as the tools of the trade are concerned, when pen-ciling, I use blue pencil and 2H pencil; when inking, I use a #3 brush and a 102 Hunt quill…and white paint when needed… if needed.

K A R L   K E S E L

"The court of Jabba the Hutt is in the midst of a drunken, raucous party. Sloppy, smelly monsters cheer and make rude noises…"

from the "Return of the Jedi" screenplay

The Max Rebo Band, featuring lead singer/dancer Sy Snootles, kept the denizens of Jabba the Hutt's palace hopping. It was Lucas himself who added Snooty's ruby-red, Mick Jagger-like lips. The music for her song was composed by John Williams, with English lyrics (later dubbed into Huttese) by Williams' son Joseph.

"I remember when *Star Wars* premiered," reflects Karl Kesel. "I was just out of high school. I could drive, drink, vote, go to war. A lot of people buying this book weren't even born then — and a lot more saw the movie when they were 'a little kid' and now have kids of their own! The phenomenon isn't fading — it's becoming ingrained. It's become part of our culture." Kesel chose Jabba's rock 'n' roll trio to illustrate because "they're wacky, and I like wacky. And Boba Fett was taken."

Kesel started drawing comics in 1984, naturally gravitating toward uncommercial characters

(AMETHST, 'MAZING MAN, etc.). He's recently illustrated a series of STAR WARS Young Adult novels, is currently writing and rendering an INDIANA JONES mini-series and is inking THE SAVAGE DRAGON ANNUAL along with various covers and back-ups for Erik Larsen's

DRAGONVERSE (Image). Additionally, Kesel became the regular writer on ADVENTURES OF SUPERMAN just in time to watch him die. ✷

Says Karl Kesel: "There's no real secrets or insights into how I draw. I just doodle around until it looks right — or until I've run out of time — and then I stop. Probably the best-kept secret about my GALAXY piece is that I didn't color it. I have a lousy color sense — I have enough trouble with black & white, thank you very much. My beautiful wife, Barbara Randall Kesel, colored it — and did a wonderful job. It's about time she got credit for it."

S A M   K I E T H

"The throne room is filled with the vilest, most grotesque creatures ever conceived in the universe. Jabba the Hutt, the leader of this nauseating crowd, is a repulsive blob of bloated fat with a maniacal grin. Chained to the horrible creature is the beautiful alien female dancer named Oola. At the foot of the dais sits an obnoxious birdlike creature, Salacious Crumb…"

from the "Return of the Jedi" screenplay

It was Topps Comics' Editor-in-Chief Jim Salicrup who suggested the vile, bloated Jabba the Hutt as a possible subject for Sam Kieth to illustrate. "Why not?" Kieth responded philosophically. "In 40 years, I'll look like that myself."

Kieth is a native Californian who learned the comic book ropes as the inker on Comico's well-received MAGE. After various other projects he hit national acclaim once again with THE SANDMAN for DC (1988). Kieth went on to illustrate EPICURUS THE SAGE and eventually wound up drawing WOLVERINE covers and stories for Marvel Comics. His own creation, THE MAXX, is published by Image Comics. ✳

If Jabba is Sidney Greenstreet, then Salacious Crumb has to be Peter Lorre. Film buff George Lucas frequently patterns his monsters after classic screen villains. It took 76 sketches before Jabba's final appearance was approved. Two tons of clay and 600 lbs. of latex later, sculptor Stuart Freeborn brought the vile gangster to three-dimensional life.

Sam Kieth enjoyed working on the STAR WARS GALAXY series because he found it challenging to try to convey the slimy texture of Jabba the Hutt with pen and ink. He also wanted to convey Jabba's size, so he added the female and the small Salacious Crumb to that card. This addition had the further advantage of giving Kieth the opportunity to draw two Salacious Crumbs (on two different cards), a character that he finds most appealing, and one that is well-suited to his rather cartoony style.

DAVID LAPHAM

"Chewie now has a little bit more of Threepio back together. One arm is connected, but the legs have yet to be attached. There is one small problem, however: It seems the Wookiee has managed to put the droid's head on backward…"

from "The Empire Strikes Back" screenplay

"I was only seven when my parents took me to see *Star Wars*," remembers David Lapham. "Wow. All little kids deserve a place like that."

Lapham, artist and co-creator of PLASM, lives in New Jersey with his wife Maria and his dog Killer. He first developed an interest in comic books at the age of eleven when he purchased his first book: DAREDEVIL, written and illustrated by Frank Miller. "It was just cool," says Lapham, "so realistic, and it had Ninjas."

One month before his wedding, Lapham began working for Valiant Comics. "Valiant was a great experience," the artist says with pride. "Every project I worked on: RAI, HARBINGER, H.A.R.D. CORPS and SHADOW-MAN, I had a hand in creatively. I even designed most of the characters. It was everything I could have hoped for, a great beginning."

Recently, David has gone on to other projects, including a trading card in Topps' GALAXY series and a SUPERMAN annual for DC. However, the majority of his energy is presently dedicated to Jim Shooter's new company Defiant. "It's so exciting…the whole crew that started Valiant is back together again, building another universe." ✳

We can practically hear Chewbacca's frustrated moans as he ponders the difficult task of putting dismembered Threepio back together again in *The Empire Strikes Back*. Since Wookiees are seven feet tall, the actor inside the furry outfit had to be equally towering…at seven feet two inches, Peter Mayhew fit the bill. "I think a Wookiee is a kind of cross between a large bear, a dog, and a monkey," explains George Lucas. "And he's very friendly until you get him riled."

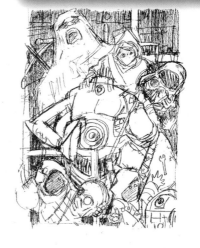

"I drew the original piece in pen and ink pretty much as I usually do," explains David Lapham. "This was the first piece I've done in color. My teacher Janet Jackson helped quite a bit. The materials used were brush, Dr. Martin's watercolor dyes, and airbrush. By the way, when the piece was finished originally, the Jawas were putting Darth Vader's head on the disassembled C-3PO (check out the pencil prelim, left). I thought it was hysterical. I don't think the *Star Wars* people appreciate my sense of humor."

MIKE LEMOS

"Suddenly the slimy alien disappears in a blinding flash of light. Han pulls his smoking gun from beneath the table as the other patrons look on in bemused amazement. Han gets up and starts out of the cantina, flipping the bartender some coins as he leaves..."

from the "Star Wars" screenplay

Greedo, a bounty hunter working for Jabba the Hutt, gets zapped. "My painting is really a story about Han Solo," explains Mike Lemos. "You're looking at his signature without seeing him, and in that, you know a little about him."

From the '60s to the '90s, Lemos has been drawing BEMs with knuckles dragging on the ground, or spacemen of one sort or another, "things invented when I was a kid frightened at what lurked under my bed or in the closet at night, good monsters to fight off the bad ones. Guess things haven't changed much."

Lemos is aggressively "pro-space" and admits that *Star Wars* was an inspiration for a whole bunch of alien concepts and stories. He's currently working on an ambitious series of "moon colony" adventures which contain, not surprisingly, dozens of newfangled aliens. "That particular project represents three years of work," adds Lemos, who confesses that "anything with tentacles, rolling eyeballs and spaceships...really makes my day." ✳

With his blaster concealed under a cantina table, Han Solo (Harrison Ford) blows away bounty hunter Greedo in this memorable moment from the original *Star Wars*. "In the first film," explains director George Lucas, "you're in a foreign environment - you don't know what's going on. (Believe it or not), it's the same for the author as it is for the audience..."

In Mike Lemos' original rough, Greedo is shot from under the cantina table, just like in the movie. This was soon changed to an above-table blast (right) to make the illustration more exciting. For the finish, Lemos utilized a combination of acrylic paint with traditional brushwork, highlighted by airbrushing.

E S T E B A N M A R O T O

"Luke and Leia crouch together in an alcove for protection as they continue to exchange fire with the troops. The Princess suddenly grabs Luke's gun and fires at a small grate in the wall next to Han, almost frying him. She jumps through the narrow opening as Han and Chewbacca look on in amazement."

from the "Star Wars" screenplay

"I would love to draw (the *Star Wars* characters) in their remote worlds far away from the limits of our galaxy," reflects Esteban Maroto, "in the deep corners of my fantasy away from this reality that saddens me with its monotony. It's a curious thing, that in a world where all is fiction — the movies — I found a sort of profound truth: nothing overcomes the illusions and excitement of a child. All of my efforts have been to reach that kind of illusion with my drawings. Someday I will get it (exactly right), and then I myself will become an excited child again."

A successful fantasy illustrator in Spain, Maroto first came to the attention of U.S. fans with splendid work for Warren's CREEPY, EERIE, VAMPIRELLA and DRACULA books. Equally interesting were his DC period (AMETHYST, ZATANNA, THE MAGICIAN, ATLANTIS CHRONICLES) and recent work for Topps (VLAD THE IMPALER). Maroto is currently rendering "wonderful women, prehistoric monsters and remote worlds" for FANTASY magazine, as well as ongoing CONAN THE BARBARIAN assignments for Marvel. ✳

Plucky Princess Leia (Carrie Fisher) literally shocks Jabba the Hutt in the prison barge sequence from *Return of the Jedi*."I wanted to do the role of Princess Leia because I wanted to have real conversations with people with bubbles on their heads," the actress explains. "Although I never read much science fiction before I made *Star Wars*, I had a kind of active space fantasy life all my own."

Esteban Maroto placed the scantily-clad Princess Leia next to her bloated master Jabba in his first rough, then decided it would be more interesting and exciting to see her atop a Dewback lizard. Maroto is a pen-and-ink line artist known for his fanciful conceptions.

CYNTHIA MARTIN

"Lando moves threateningly toward Han. Suddenly, he throws his arms around his startled, long-lost friend and embraces him. The two old friends enjoy an unexpected reunion, laughing and chuckling..."

from "The Empire Strikes Back" screenplay

They spoke about it in *The Empire Strikes Back*, but we never saw it — until now: Han Solo wins the Millennium Falcon from Lando Calrissian in a card game.

"I chose to avoid showing Han Solo's face, attractive though it may be, and focused instead on the winning card that he's holding in his hand," Cynthia Martin explains. "That really tells the whole story. I threw in a few cantina aliens, figuring these guys would probably turn up in gambling dens across the galaxy, as semi-humorous spectators."

The artist readily admits that *Star Wars* had an awesome effect on her as a young adult, and consequently as an illustrator. "Seeing the movie when I was 15 was like being transcended onto another level of being," she remembers. "What a ride!"

Martin's impressive work includes the original STAR WARS comic for Marvel, a PUNISHER graphic novel, JASON GOES TO HELL for Topps, and ELVIRA for Claypool Comics. ✳

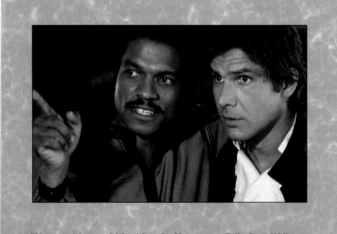

"Han and I are old buddies," offers actor Billy Dee Williams. "He's the one who 'stole' my ship. We've had this kind of thing going on for years, though...hassling, running around doing numbers. At one point or another, I just take off and start my own thing (a mining operation on the Cloud City of Bespin). I get tired of being 'out there'..."

Cynthia Martin experimented with a couple of different pencil compositions before settling on the "winning card" approach, which dictated the style and ultimate content of the piece. For her finish, Martin used gouache to achieve the proper lighting and mood.

MICHAEL MIGNOLA

"The Sandpeople, or Tusken Raiders as they're sometimes called, speak in a course barbaric language. One of these marginally human creatures raises a long ominous laser rifle and points it at Luke's approaching landspeeder..."

from the "Star Wars" screenplay

Mike Mignola's Sandperson (or Tusken Raider) reflects the artist's feelings about *Star Wars*: "Robot junk, dirty spaceships and cool-looking aliens — everything a 16-year old kid could have wanted! I'll never forget seeing the original theatrical trailer... My friends and I sat there stunned! We'd never seen spaceships move so fantastically in a movie."

Mignola jumped at the chance to render a *Star Wars* entity. "The Tusken Raiders looked so great, and sounded so weird," he observes. "Waving that big stick over its head, making that ungodly sound. I've been haunted by the howling of the Tusken Raiders ever since..."

Mignola began comics work in the early '80s, penciling such titles as ROCKET RACCOON, THE HULK and ALPHA FLIGHT. In the ten years since, he's rendered COSMIC ODYSSEY and GOTHAM BY GASLIGHT for DC, Marvel's WOLVERINE, and BRAM STOKER'S DRACULA for Topps, among many others. His 1993 creation HELLBOY was an immediate hit for Dark Horse, and Mike also found time to depict scenes from *The Bride of Frankenstein* for Topps UNIVERSAL MONSTERS card series. ✷

Portrait of a fearsome Tusken Raider who assaults Luke on Tatooine in the original *Star Wars*. Back in 1976, cargo planes and oversized trans-European moving vans brought thousands of pieces of equipment and props to the remote desert of Tunisia, which doubled for Tatooine. During the first week of filming, a sandstorm swept through the area. The entire crew wore specially supplied goggles, and cameras had to be rigorously cleaned out every night.

Mike Mignola went from a trio of Tusken Raiders to a single dramatic figure as his pencil designs progressed. His finished illustration is a combination of inked linework and water color.

MOEBIUS

"Threepio is in the midst of a long, animated speech in the Ewok's squeaky native tongue.

Threepio points several times at the Rebel group and pantomimes a short history of the

Galactic Civil War, mimicking the explosion and rocket sounds, imitating Imperial walkers..."

from the "Return of the Jedi" screenplay

"When *Star Wars* first came out," remembers Jean 'Moebius' Giraud, "I was ecstatic because it was exactly the kind of science fiction I love...and I draw. I chose to spotlight C-3PO in this piece because I thought he was one of the film's most interesting characters. I mean this not from a story standpoint, but from a visual standpoint. Darth Vader is also very interesting, very powerful, but maybe a little more conventional. For some reason I was more drawn towards a character expressing a lighter, more positive emotion. You can tell that the other characters have been added almost as an afterthought."

Lauded in France for his luminous fantasy illustrations, Moebius has won every major international comics award and has even been honored on a stamp! Significant work includes ARZACK (1975), THE AIRTIGHT GARAGE (1979), HEAVY METAL contributions and Marvel's SILVER SURFER: PARABLE, with Stan Lee. Among his most recent work for comics are

THE MADWOMAN OF THE SACRED HEART, a story written by Alexandro Jodorowsky, which has appeared in DARK HORSE PRESENTS; and STEL, the fourth graphic novel in the Aedena Cycle, which will be released in 1994 as a graphic novel by Marvel (as MOEBIUS #9). He is currently working on THE MAN FROM THE CLOUD, a sequel to THE AIRTIGHT GARAGE. ✳

"You're always surprised (with the characters you create). In film it's even more dramatic than writing, because eventually you actually take a person and stick him into that character, and that person brings with him an enormous package of reality. C-3PO is just a chunk of plastic, and without Tony Daniels in there, it just isn't anything. I had a different idea for that character originally. I wanted him to be more of a used-car dealer, slick-o, oily...but that character inhabited that costume so strongly, because of what Tony had done, that I couldn't change it," explains George Lucas.

Moebius' C-3PO illustration was drawn mostly with acrylics, with a little gouache to add highlights. The original art measures 7" x 12".

JEROME MOORE

"The shuttle's ramp lowers and the Emperor's Royal Guards come out and create a lethal perimeter. The assembled troops move to rigid attention with a momentous snap. Then, in the huge silence which follows, the Emperor appears…"

from the "Return of the Jedi" screenplay

Jerome Moore on the Emperor's Royal Guard: "Silent, statuesque, and utterly mysterious, this crimson-robed sextet appears only briefly in Episode Six. Nevertheless, theirs is an intimidating presence as befits their station. Each glimpse of the Imperial Guard, with their regal carriage and stoicism, only serves to pique my curiosity. At once, both colorful contrast and compliment to our ebon Sith Lord, I wonder just how formidable they are. What is the true depth of their loyalty? Do they get cable in those helmets?"

Compelled by the Force to graduate from New York's High School of Art and Design, Moore almost immediately began working for DC Comics, illustrating the company's top superhero characters. Not long ago he made his mark as cover artist for Innovation's LOST IN SPACE, DC's STAR TREK titles and Malibu's STAR TREK: DEEP SPACE NINE. Currently Moore is working with his partner Hank Kanalz on the upcoming MASQUERADE and the creator-owned RUNAWAY for Malibu's ULTRAVERSE . ✳

When Emperor Palpatine arrives on the new Death Star for an inspection, he is preceded by his personal guards…sinister, imposing figures cloaked in red. All of the costumes for *Return of the Jedi* were designed by Aggie Guerard Rodgers and Nilo Rodis-Jamero.

The arrival of Palpatine and his court: It took a couple of preliminary pencil renderings before Jerome Moore was convinced he was on the right track. The final version (right) was "actually one of my least favorite design ideas for the cards, but it was the simplest and the most direct," he feels.

J
O
N

J

M
U
T
H

"Luke speaks into the comlink as a medical droid works on his hand. A metalized type of bandage has been wrapped around Luke's wrist. The medical droid makes some adjustments in a tiny electronic unit, then pricks each one of Luke's fingers…"

from "The Empire Strikes Back" screenplay

"The robots in *Star Wars* were like children, but they were also slightly menacing," concludes Jon J Muth. "If Too-Onebee (the robo-surgeon from *The Empire Strikes Back*) had found Luke's lost hand he would have been fascinated."

Born in 1960 in Cincinnati, Ohio and originally trained as a painter, Muth's graphic novels include MOONSHADOW, DRACULA-A SYMPHONY IN MOONLIGHT AND NIGHTMARES, HAVOC & WOLVERINE - MELTDOWN, THE MYTHOLOGY OF AN ABANDONED CITY, FRITZ LANG'S M and THE MYSTERY PLAY, with Grant Morrison. Soon to be released projects include STANISLAW LEM'S THE STAR DIARIES and THE PROTECTING VEIL.

A book of Muth's paintings, drawings and ideas entitled VANITAS was released in 1991 by Tundra Publishing Ltd. The artist has participated in exhibits across the United States and his work is in numerous private and corporate collections here as well as in Europe and Japan. ✳

Surgeon droids are commonplace in the Rebel Alliance. Too-Onebee provided Luke Skywalker with an artificial hand at the end of *The Empire Strikes Back*; earlier in that same film he nursed the young Jedi back to health after a nasty Wampa attack on Hoth. The relationship between man and machine has always fascinated George Lucas. If his *Star Wars* saga is about anything, it's about the triumph of the human spirit in the face of technological adversity.

"The tensions created by the 'machines which can think' in *Star Wars* was exciting to me," comments Jon J Muth. "I liked the personalities that George Lucas gave all of the hardware. When he chose not to give them a personality, we were greeted with something strange, alien, usually fearsome." Muth's Too-Onebee was rendered in oil, graphite, charcoal and silverpoint on prepared board.

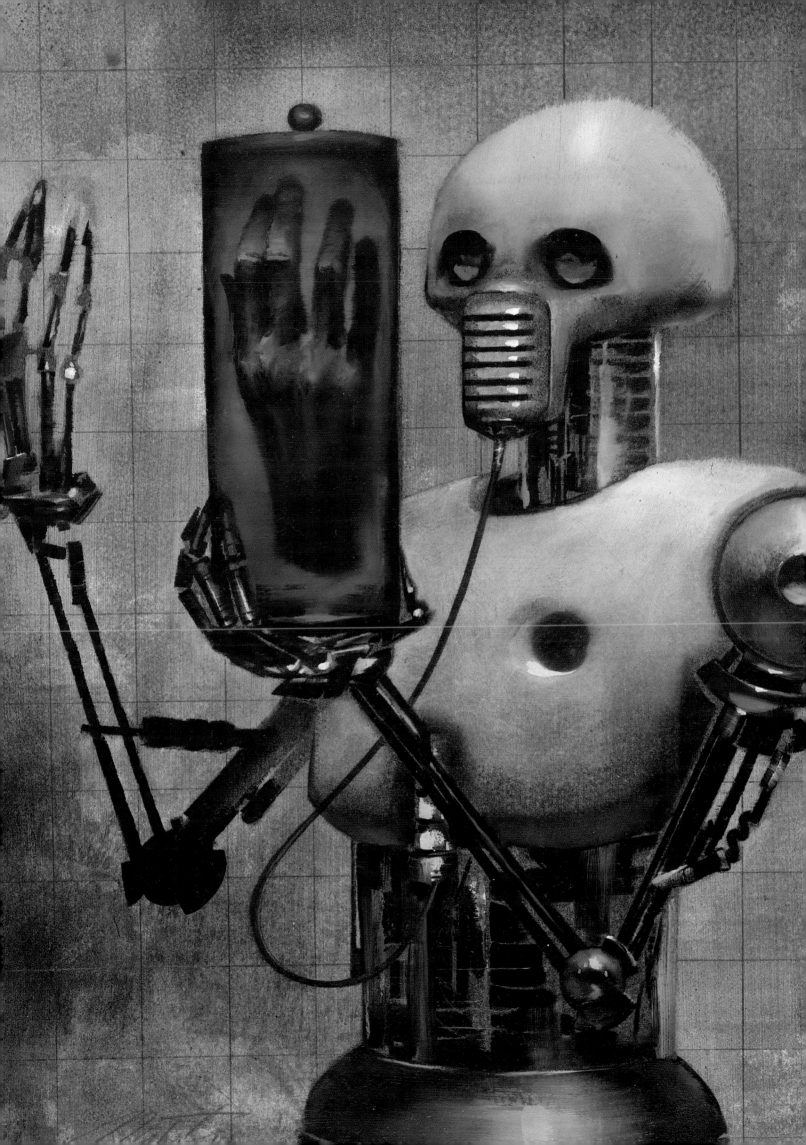

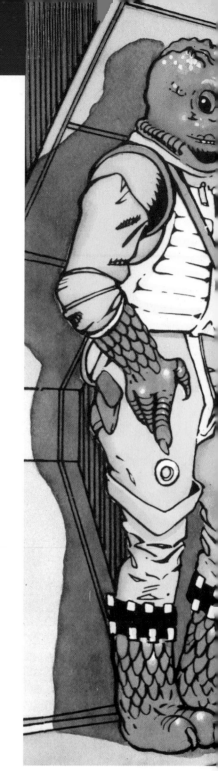

MARK NELSON

"Before Vader stands a bizarre array of galactic fortune hunters: Bossk, a slimy, tentacled monster with two huge, bloodshot eyes; Zuckuss and Dengar, two battle-scarred, mangy human types; IG-88, a battered, tarnished chrome war droid; and Boba Fett, a man in a weapon-covered armored space suit…"

from "The Empire Strikes Back" screenplay

"One of the facets of *Star Wars* that always intrigued me," recalls Mark Nelson, "was the amazing array of extraterrestrial lifeforms that George Lucas and his people dreamed up for us. If I had my druthers, I'd be drawing critters and beasties all the time…and the more outlandish the better."

"I remember seeing *Star Wars* when it was first released in the theaters," Nelson continues, "being mesmerized throughout the film, and as the final credits rolled, thinking: this film has action, adventure, heroes, villains, story; it's creative, direct and honest. I want more! Luckily, *Star Wars* was just the first taste of what was to come."

Beginning his comics career in the early '80s, Nelson's works include ALIENS, NIGHTBREED, HELLRAISER and many others. He is currently involved in Topps' updated comic book version of the classic sci-fi card series, MARS ATTACKS. ✻

A successful penciler and inker, Mark Nelson had his enjoyable work cut out for him with this STAR WARS GALAXY assignment. The self-confessed "creature" fanatic jammed six unearthly entities into one trading card — and had a ball doing it.

Another view of the loathsome bounty hunters assembled by Darth Vader aboard his starship, the Executor. Creatures , monsters and robots have been popular in motion pictures since the birth of the medium. George Lucas populated his *Star Wars* galaxy with some of the strangest lifeforms ever seen on the screen. Stuart Freeborn, Phil Tippett, Rick Baker and Ron Cobb are just some of the professional monster-makers engaged to fulfill Lucas' nightmarish visions.

E A R L   N O R E M

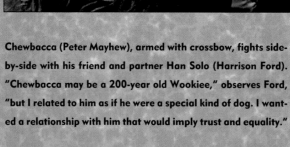

"Chewbacca is an eight-foot-tall savage-looking creature resembling a huge grey bushbaby monkey with fierce baboon-like fangs. His large blue eyes dominate a fur-covered face and soften his otherwise awesome appearance. He is a two-hundred year-old Wookiee and a sight to behold…"

from the "Star Wars" screenplay

"Gary Gerani told me he read somewhere that George Lucas always wanted to see the Wookiees on their native planet, doing some kind of tribal war dance around a bonfire," recalls Earl Norem. "Gary thought I'd be perfect for the assignment. I hope George approves!"

Norem, the gentleman's gentleman of fantasy illustration, has worked for companies as diverse as Marvel Comics and Reader's Digest. His masterful paintings for SAVAGE WORD OF CONAN, RAMPAGING HULK and DINOSAURS ATTACK! are among the most respected in the field. Currently, Earl is preparing new CONAN covers for Marvel as well as a trio of trading card paintings. Among them is the Wendigo, an abominable snowman-like monster who in some ways resembles an ill-tempered, distant cousin of the Wookiees. ✳

Chewbacca (Peter Mayhew), armed with crossbow, fights side-by-side with his friend and partner Han Solo (Harrison Ford). "Chewbacca may be a 200-year old Wookiee," observes Ford, "but I related to him as if he were a special kind of dog. I wanted a relationship with him that would imply trust and equality."

Before the "Wookiee war dance" suggestion, Earl Norem originally toyed with illustrating the Imperial Walkers from *Empire* (artist Russell Walks pretty much followed through with this concept — see page 120). Norem mostly uses acrylics for his creations, occasionally applying pro-white for highlights.

A L L E N N U N I S

"Jabba stares at the silver ball, which begins to glow in the bounty hunter's hand. The room has fallen into a tense hush. Jabba stares at the bounty hunter malevolently until a sly grin creeps across his vast mouth and he begins to laugh..."

from the "Return of the Jedi" screenplay

"George Lucas is like the kid on the block with the best toys," says Allen Nunis with a grin. "It's always fun to play in George's backyard!"

Nunis personally selected the subject of his GALAXY illustration. "I feel, next to Boba Fett's outfit, Leia's bounty hunter costume (from *Return of the Jedi*) is one of the best of the series. I did my best to capture every detail and nuance...even her little bomb was interesting to draw."

A protégé of Al Williamson, Nunis has spent five years providing artwork for the role-playing game industry, including the STAR WARS RPG from West End Games. Recent projects include cover work on the CLASSIC STAR WARS reprint, an ALIENS mini-series (both for Dark Horse) and JASON GOES TO HELL (inks) for Topps Comics. ✳

It's all an act: the mighty Wookiee Chewbacca (Peter Mayhew), captured by a short-but-formidable bounty hunter named Boushh, is presented to Jabba the Hutt and held at bomb-point. Actually, it's Princess Leia (Carrie Fisher) posing as the resourceful Boushh. A few years after *Jedi*, Warren Beatty's *Dick Tracy* would disguise Breathless (Madonna) with a similar voice distortion.

Princess Leia disguised as the sinister-sounding bounty hunter Boushh was a favorite subject of Allen Nunis. The artist works exclusively in black and white line art, using crow quill pen and brush.

J
A
S
O
N
P
A
L
M
E
R

"At the side of the pit, an iron door rumbles upward and a giant, fanged Rancor emerges. The monster turns and starts for Luke. The young Jedi dashes away just ahead of the monster's swipe at him, and picks up the long arm-bone of an earlier victim…"

from the "Return of the Jedi" screenplay

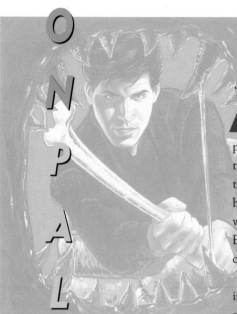

"**A**lthough no match for our Jedi," states Jason Palmer, "the Rancor was perhaps the most fearsome creature to come out of the *Star Wars* trilogy. Ten tons of rage and hunger, it's a mutant creature who unwittingly serves as Executioner for Jabba and his court's entertainment.

"When Luke faces this abomination he realizes that it isn't evil, but that it has been driven mad by years of confinement and abuse. By slaying this 'dragon,' Luke wants to put the pitiful creature out if its misery, as well as save his own skin."

Born and raised in Los Angeles, Palmer began working professionally in comics in 1991, painting covers for LOST IN SPACE, THE GREEN HORNET, STAR TREK trade paperbacks, DEBT OF HONOR and THE STARLOST. Recent assignments include penciling covers for DC's STAR TREK: THE NEXT GENERATION and a series of STAR WARS posters for Hasson Productions. ✴

The ferocious Rancor was in actuality an 18" puppet, "a cross between a gorilla and a potato" according to Master of Monsters Phil Tippett. The multi-fanged creature required three operators and was filmed in slow motion so its movements would appear awesome and inescapable on the screen.

Explains Jason Palmer: "This piece was painted in acrylics on illustration board, which I first primed with gesso. Gesso is like a cross between paint and a fine plaster. On the areas with rocks I swirled the gesso very thick. Later, this texture was accented to give a stony effect. After the board was primed, my original pencil drawing was transferred. The paint was put on with a wash, then airbrushed. Once the colors and values were set, details were worked in with airbrush, brush and colored pencils.

G E O R G E   P E R E Z

"The Rancor moves past Luke, and as the Gamorrean Guard continues to scramble, the Rancor picks him up and pops him into its salivating jaws. A few screams, and the guard is swallowed with a gulp. The audience cheers and laughs at the guard's fate..."

from the "Return of the Jedi" screenplay

"*S*tar Wars introduced a whole new logic to drawing SF hardware," observes George Perez. "Previously, most spaceships tended to be boxy — horizontal and vertical. Lucas made them exciting and aerodynamically captivating. Also, the introduction of *Star Wars* brought computer enhanced special effects into the movie mainstream. Now, anything you can put on paper, in a comic book, can be put on the motion picture screen...only we can do it cheaper!"

A comics pro for 18 years, Perez has done considerable work for both Marvel and DC, including THE AVENGERS, THE FANTASTIC FOUR, THE NEW TEEN TITANS, CRISIS ON INFINITE EARTHS, WONDER WOMAN and INFINITY GAUNTLET. Recent accomplishments include HULK: FUTURE IMPERFECT, GLADIATOR, JURASSIC PARK (inks) for Topps, SAX AND VIOLENS (Epic/Marvel) and BREAKTHRU (Malibu). ✳

Like many of the monsters developed for George Lucas' dream universe, the Gamorrean Guard went through a series of significant changes in concept and design. Although always ugly, he was at first more simian-like. Dave Carson of ILM reworked Joe Johnston's original renderings and came up with a bloated monster that Lucas would forever refer to as "the pig" or "the pig-guard."

"I felt that the Gamorrean Guard would be quite intimidating in extreme close-up," offers George Perez. "Besides, comic art is one of the few places you can make a rubber mask look like the real thing!" Perez is a pen and ink artist by necessity, as his double-jointed fingers can't control a paint brush.

G E O R G E P R A T T

"His face is obscured by his flowing black robes and grotesque breath mask, which stands out next to the fascist white armored suits of the Imperial stormtroopers. Everyone instinctively backs away from the imposing warrior and a deathly quiet sweeps through the Rebel troops..."

from the "Star Wars" screenplay

"**I**n a world where the success of a movie is based on how many people you can waste with a single bullet and how much of a wall one person's blood will cover, it's nice to remember the *Star Wars* films," observes George Pratt. "*Star Wars* liberated science fiction movies in that the special effects opened up new frontiers, but at the same time it also boxed the genre in because of those same effects. Fortunately, the *Star Wars* epics had stories to back them up, worlds and characters rich with histories and possibilities. The effects were just icing on the cake. Absolutely wonderful!"

Pratt's comics-style work has appeared in Marvel's EPIC ILLUSTRATED, HEAVY METAL and EAGLE magazines. He is currently writing and rendering a new novel, SEE YOU IN HELL, as well as illustrating Gabor Garabas' poems of the Holocaust, FIND ME A VOICE.

A successful painter, Pratt's creations have been showcased in a number of prestigious museums. ✳

It took two actors to portray the Dark Lord of the Sith: David Prowse, the undefeated weightlifting champion who was physically inside the awesome costume; and James Earl Jones, the celebrated Shakespearean actor who lent his imposing voice to the character. "After the first movie," recalls George Lucas, "we really weren't sure where to take Darth Vader. He had become very popular, and I really wasn't prepared for that. Finally, we decided to stick to the original story [with Vader being Luke's father]."

Explains George Pratt: "I generally don't work in any specific media, shifting from pen and ink to oils to acrylics to watercolor to printmaking depending on the needs of the piece at hand. For the Darth Vader card, I used printmaking. A monotype is a print pulled from a very thin oil painting which is executed on an etching plate or a piece of plexiglass. The painting is then run through an etching press, or reversed impression, thus the term: monotype."

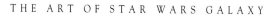

J
O
E

Q
U
E
S
A
D
A

"The young warrior grabs for his lightsabre as he spins around, looking for the speaker. Mysteriously standing right in front of Luke is a strange, bluish creature, not more than two feet tall. The wizened little thing is dressed in rags. It motions toward Luke's sword..."

from "The Empire Strikes Back" screenplay

What prompted Joe Quesada to render the Jedi Master Yoda? "He looks like my cat!"

Remarkably, Quesada began his comics career just over two years ago (1991), as a colorist for Valiant's NINTENDO comics. Since that time, he's gone on to pencil some of the most important books and covers for the industry's largest publishers. His accomplishments include THE RAY 6-issue mini-series for DC Comics, the BATMAN/SWORD OF AZREAL 4-issue mini-series (also for DC) and monthly penciling duties for Marvel's X-FACTOR.

Some of the artist's most striking creations have been the SOLAR covers he continues to do for Valiant. Other projects include X-O MANOWAR #0, as well as a chapter of the celebrated Valiant/Image DEATHMATE crossover. Through the course of his brief tenure in the business, Quesada has done trading card art for both Upper Deck and Topps. The illustrator "desperately needs a day off," and knows Mike Mignola personally. ✴

With Ben Kenobi pretty much out of the picture in EMPIRE, young Luke needed some kind of Jedi trainer. Enter Yoda, the Jedi Master who previously instructed Ben. Yoda was a ground-breaking puppet developed by Stuart Freeborn...who took pains to give the little gnome "Albert Einstein eyes." Yoda's complicated, life-like movements were controlled by Frank (Miss Piggy) Oz, who also supplied the creature's voice.

Joe Quesada's pencil portrait of Yoda on Dagobah was inked by industry great Al Williamson. Beyond comics, Quesada is also a talented musician/singer/songwriter whose well-established New York band is currently being considered by major recording labels.

P. CRAIG RUSSELL

"Bib Fortuna appears out of the gloom. He speaks to Luke as they approach each other, but Luke doesn't stop and Bib must reverse his direction and hurry alongside the young Jedi in order to carry on the conversation. Several other guards fall in behind them in the darkness..."

from the "Return of the Jedi" screenplay

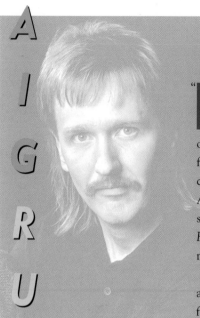

"**D**espite his 'marginal' status," explains P. Craig Russell, "Bib Fortuna is one of those characters who's fun to draw because of all the care put into his original design. And although he's only on-screen for about ten minutes in *Return of the Jedi*, he's extremely memorable."

A twenty year comics veteran, Russell established a name for himself at Marvel and went on to win acclaim for ELRIC, his stylish adaptations of operas by Wagner (PARSIFAL) and Mozart (THE MAGIC FLUTE), as well as literary classics such as Kipling's JUNGLE BOOK stories and SALOME. Recent work includes a second volume of Oscar Wilde fairy tales for NBM, a SLAUGHTERHOUSE FIVE adaptation for Byron Preiss Visual Publications and a new ELRIC comics series for Topps. ✳

The grotesque Bib Fortuna (Michael Carter, right) stands beside his bloated slug of a master, Jabba the Hutt. The throne-room sequence from *Return of the Jedi* took almost a month to film. A crew of 90 were required, including 19 puppeteers, 9 mime artists and 42 extras. Cool air was blown into the various monster masks with ordinary hair dryers, and Jabba - literally the biggest star of this scene - had a make-up artist assigned to him full time.

The ornate, strangely comforting, fairy tale-like style of P. Craig Russell was well-received in a field (comics) traditionally obsessed with muscle-bound costumed heroes and vulgar villains. "My advice to the young artist is stick to your vision, your passion, no matter how uncommercial some people tell you it is," says Russell.

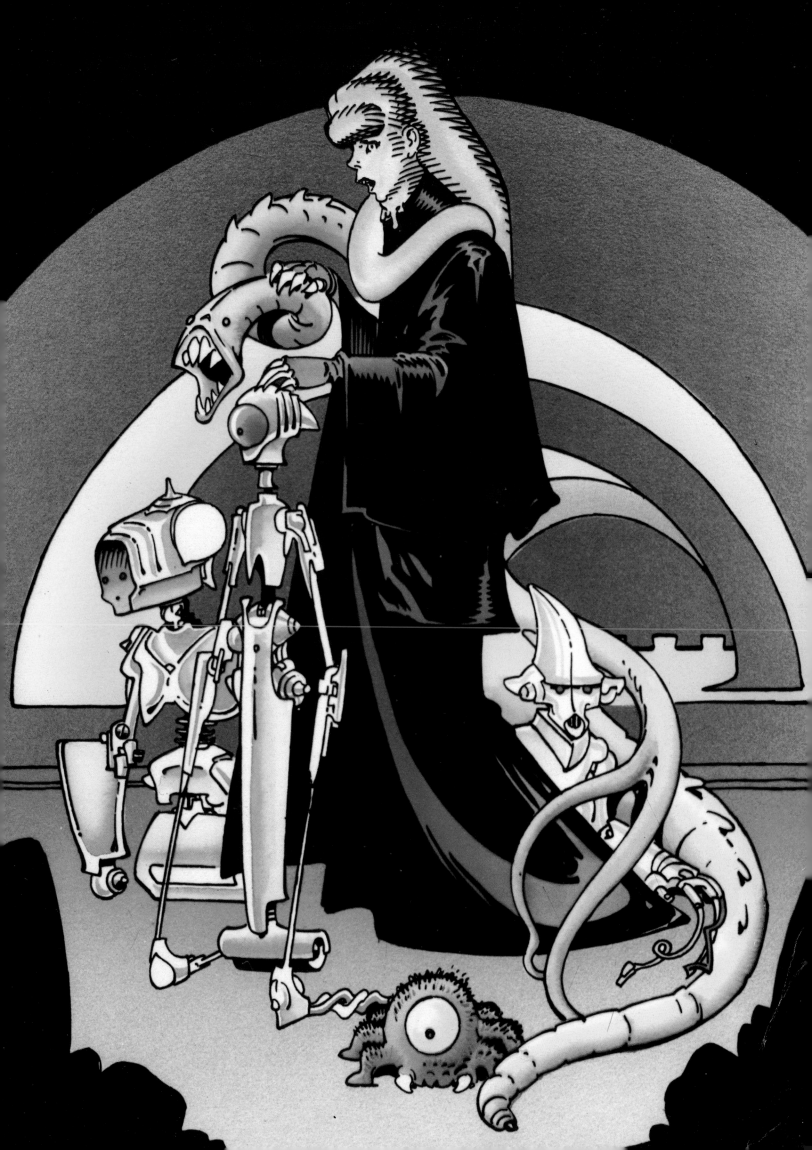

MARK SCHULTZ

"Luke watches the distant Tusken Raider through his electrobinoculars. Suddenly something huge moves in front of his field of view. Before Luke or Threepio can react, a large, gruesome Tusken Raider looms over them…"

from the "Star Wars" screenplay

"All aficionados of science fiction and fantasy owe a debt of gratitude to George Lucas," declares Mark Schultz. "With *Star Wars*, he proved to a moribund Hollywood dream factory that science fiction will be popularly supported…so long as it is well-made. I always enjoyed the early scenes of Luke on Tatooine because it became obvious to me during these that Lucas had a real understanding and love for the myths and conventions of western and adventure films."

A longtime frustrated cartoonist, Schultz left the commercial illustration field in 1986 to take the plunge into comics. His popular creation for Kitchen Sink Press, XENOZOIC TALES, evolved into the equally-successful CADILLACS AND DINOSAURS, DINOSAUR SHAMAN and TIME IN OVERDRIVE. It also spawned the *Cadillacs and Dinosaurs* animated TV series on CBS, as well as a monthly CADILLACS companion comic from Topps. ✳

"Luke's landspeeder was a real problem," notes former Lucas associate Charles Lippincott. "Ultimately John Stears got a tri-wheel vehicle and completely redesigned it. In some shots it really looks as if it's floating on air. There was no problem with tire tracks because it was rarely used with the wheels. The problem was that we couldn't use a hovercraft because it would have tossed up a cloud of sand and caused all sorts of hell."

"In my storytelling and drawing, I am a traditionalist," notes Mark Schultz. "I need to work from a full, complete script. I work out my layouts and do tight pencils with an H or 2H lead, and ink with the good old dependable Windsor & Newton series 7 #2 brush. I slightly water my ink to keep it flowing smoothly."

B I L L   S I E N K I E W I C Z

"Slowly, hesitantly, Luke removes the mask from his father's face. There beneath the scars is an elderly man. His eyes do not focus. But the dying man smiles at the sight before him…"

from the "Return of the Jedi" screenplay

"Seeing *Star Wars* for the first time was an incredible experience," recalls Bill Sienkiewicz. "What I found so compelling about the character of Darth Vader, aside from the obvious visual clues that fairly hissed malevolence (the W.W.II German helmet-derived styling of Darth's own headpiece, to the in-your-face simplicity of his black costume), were the elements of tragedy and human weakness in his persona of Anakin Skywalker, the man beneath the mask. When unmasked, he appeared ravaged, and beaten, as if he had been held hostage by the costume of Darth Vader itself, and by the evil it represented. This costume served as both armor and prison, as life support system and parasitic functional ID: the epitome of the Dark Side. I chose to show Darth Vader as both the inscrutable force of darkness, and as the frail, all too human, man within."

A comics professional since 1978, Sienkiewicz also designs and illustrates magazines and record albums. Comics credits include FANTASTIC FOUR, ELECTRA: ASSASSIN, MOON KNIGHT, STRAY TOASTERS, MOBY DICK, FIVE GLORIES and his most recent project for Random House:

Redemption: the soul of the *Star Wars* saga. "The concept of the film originally was that the people were the most important thing," notes producer Gary Kurtz. "The technology was just there. Like, you go out and get into your car and drive home. We didn't want to get involved trying to explain how things function, because it's fantasy. We really don't relate to science on any level…people are the important thing."

VOODOO CHILD, a visual biography of Jimi Hendrix. Sienkiewicz also rendered sequential scenes from the 1933 classic *The Invisible Man* for Topps' UNIVERSAL MONSTERS card set. ✳

Bill Sienkiewicz's original pencil rough reveals a bit more of The Man in The Iron Helmet. The final painting was accomplished with watercolor, acrylics "and sweat," says the artist.

"Vader and Ben Kenobi continue their powerful duel. As they hit their lightsabres together, lightning flashes on impact. Troopers look on in interest as the old Jedi and the Dark Lord of the Sith fight…"

from the "Star Wars" screenplay

**W
A
L
T
E
R

S
I
M
O
N
S
O
N**

"I still think that one of the niftiest moments I ever sat through in a movie was during the first *Star Wars* film, when the Millennium Falcon made its initial jump into hyperspace," recollects Walter Simonson. "I was at the Loews Astor Plaza theater in New York, a really big theater, and that jump took everyone's breath away! A wonderful bit of business!"

Simonson began working professionally as an artist in 1972. He became a writer in '79 with Marvel's BATTLESTAR GALACTICA book. Since then, he's written or drawn everything from MANHUNTER to SUPERMAN to THOR to ROBOCOP VS. THE TERMINATOR to the original comics adaptation of ALIEN.

Recently, Simonson adapted the *Jurassic Park* screenplay for the Topps Comics four-issue series, scripted and drew CYBERFORCE #0 for Image, and is currently working on a new STAR SLAMMERS limited series to be published in 1994 by Malibu Comics. ✳

"I did all the sword fighting," recalls David "Darth Vader" Prowse. "Alec Guinness did it as well. We rehearsed it for about two weeks. It was actually filmed in three specific sequences. The main problems were that every time the swords (lightsabers) touched, they broke. So, of course, all of that scene was done with the swords hardly touching at all…"

"There isn't much mystery to working with pen and ink, as was true for this particular drawing," explains Walter Simonson. "But I will say that two of the most interesting challenges of this piece were composing a picture that would show relatively large figures of both protagonists in a small format, and rendering the textural element of Obi-Wan's cloak and Vader's costume."

BULL'S-EYING A WOMP RAT

"The low-ceilinged room is full of starpilots, navigators, and a sprinkling of R2-type robots. Everyone is listening intently to what Dodonna is saying. Luke is sitting next to Wedge Antilles, a hot shot pilot about sixteen years old…"

from the "Star Wars" screenplay

Explains Ken Steacy: "*Star Wars* was such a treat for a young artist…I felt as if I had been waiting for it since I was a kid. Years later I still enjoy watching the trilogy, now with my children. The scene I chose to depict is based on a throwaway line Luke delivers late in the first film — 'I used to bull's-eye womp rats in my T-16 back home and they're not much bigger than two meters' — which for some reason struck a chord. I knew what a T-16 was: Luke toys with a model of one early in the film, but what the hell was a 'womp rat'? Well, now we know! Thanks, George… I hope I got it right!"

Writer/illustrator Ken Steacy has been producing full-color sequential narratives and cover paintings for over fifteen years now. He has worked with every major comics publisher and has depicted practically every major character you could name, including Luke Skywalker (during a brief stint on the STAR WARS comic book for Marvel).

Steacy is currently engaged at Sanctuary Woods Multimedia Corporation, having a blast producing THE AWESOME ADVENTURES OF VICTOR VECTOR & YONDO, an interactive CD-ROM series. ✳

From the original *Star Wars*: Luke Skywalker (Mark Hamill) toys with his model of a T-16 as Threepio (Anthony Daniels) and Artoo (Kenny Baker) look on. Ultimately, the vehicle turned up in *Return of the Jedi* as the craft that transports Emperor Palpatine to the newly-constructed Death Star.

Says Ken Steacy: "My technique is fairly straightforward: after composing a number of small roughs I redraw the image at working size (usually 10" x 15") on bond paper with colored pencils. I trace this drawing onto Strathmore 2-ply bristol (either plate or vellum surface depending on how much texture I want) on my lightsaber — uh, I mean lightbox! I then use my trusty Iwata HP-B airbrush and Pelikan inks & Badger air-opaques (with various hard and soft masks) to establish the mid-range values and color scheme. I finish the shadows and highlights with acrylics applied with a Windsor & Newton series 7 #4 brush, then frantically call Federal Express to come and get it!"

BRIAN STELFREEZE

"The fragment breaks loose with a snap, sending Luke tumbling head over heels. He sits up and sees a twelve-inch three-dimensional hologram of Leia Organa, the Rebel senator, being projected from the face of little Artoo. Luke becomes intrigued by the beautiful young girl…"

from the "Star Wars" screenplay

"When I first saw *Star Wars*, I thought it was the first true comic book movie," observes Brian Stelfreeze. "Princess Leia was a great character because she got away from the 'helpless heroine' cliché found in most fantasy literature of this kind."

After years of commercial art and product illustration, Stelfreeze took a crack at the comics field in 1988 with a three-issue mini-series entitled PSI-COPS, published by Comics Interview. Since then he's done extraordinary work for Marvel, DC and Dark Horse (GROUND ZERO).

Of his second GALAXY illustration, Stelfreeze says, "To me, Boba Fett is visually the most interesting character in the entire *Star Wars* universe. He was super-bad, truly-ominous…a *High Plains Drifter* kind of guy who wasn't intimidated by Darth Vader."

Stelfreeze's imaginative compositions and unique color choices have earned him a legion of admirers. Notable covers include THE SHADOW OF THE BAT for DC, the fetching She-Hulk rendering that adorns MARVEL SWIMSUIT issue #1, and issue #0 of ZORRO for Topps Comics. ✱

Princess Leia (Carrie Fisher) aims her blaster at Imperial enemies in the original *Star Wars*. "I wanted a princess in my space adventure," remembers George Lucas, "but I didn't want her to be a passive damsel in distress." Later, in *Return of the Jedi*, bounty hunter Boba Fett (Jeremy Bulloch) clashes with Luke Skywalker's lightsaber in the prison barge sequence.

Brian Stelfreeze uses the same painting method employed by the Flemish masters, but with acrylics instead of oil. "First I lay down a tone value," the artist explains, either paynes gray or sepia. I wash in my transparent colors, and the tone creates all of my shadows and darkened areas. Finally, highlights are built up with opaques."

**D
A
V
E**

**S
T
E
V
E
N
S**

"The tremendous heat of two huge twin suns settles on a lone figure, Luke Skywalker, a farm boy with heroic aspirations who looks much younger than his eighteen years. His shaggy hair and baggy tunic give him the air of a simple but lovable lad with a prize-winning smile..."

from the "Star Wars" screenplay

"The portrait study of Luke (for STAR WARS GALAXY) was originally drawn in the winter of 1979," explains Dave Stevens, "and included in a group of 'audition drawings' submitted to Lucasfilm for the STAR WARS Sunday Strip."

Stevens, best known for his creation THE ROCKETEER, also wrote and drew two complete Sunday pages at the request of Lucasfilm. He returned the following summer (1980) to assist artist Rick Hoberg in ghosting several weeks of STAR WARS dailies.

A fan favorite for several years now, Stevens is currently illustrating his own novel, THE MAD WORLD OF MIMI RODAN. Other upcoming projects include new ROCKETEER compilations, BETTY PAGE prints and statuettes and VAMPIRELLA covers for Harris. Stevens is also designing photographic covers for CULT MOVIES magazine. ✷

Escaping from the Death Star, Luke Skywalker (Mark Hamill) tries not to get cocky as he wards off attacks from Imperial TIE fighters. "When I was seven or eight," recalls Hamill, "it suddenly dawned on me that some people actually make a living making monster and science fiction movies. Since then, I always knew that making those kinds of movies is what I'd have to be doing when I grew up. And here I am..."

Dave Stevens' original "wide-eyed Luke" rendering was dressed up with colored shapes for its STAR WARS GALAXY presentation. "I work very deliberately," explains the illustrator, "and never take short-cuts. I go into a job thinking about what I can bring to it that will make it special. And I won't allow the work to be compromised by time constrictions"

W I L L I A M S T O U T

"A strange little furry face with huge black eyes comes slowly into view. The creature is an Ewok, by the name of Wicket. He seems somewhat puzzled, and prods Leia with a spear. Leia sits up and stares at the three-foot-high Ewok. She tries to figure out where she is and what has happened…"

from the "Return of the Jedi" screenplay

"I believe that the Ewoks may have been inspired in part by the amazing African Pygmies," suggests William Stout. "I wanted to try to capture the dignity of one of the so-called primitive races that lives in harmony with nature, a harmony that thus far seems to elude our more 'civilized' society."

Stout's breathtaking natural history studies have been exhibited in some of the world's most important museums. He's an internationally-known motion picture designer (*First Blood, Conan the Barbarian, Masters of the Universe,* among many others) in addition to being an award-winning comics artist. Stout recently rendered the cover for an all-dinosaur issue of RAY BRADBURY COMICS (#1), for Topps, and hopes to contribute to the company's new CADILLACS AND DINOSAURS comic book series.

Incidentally, Stout traveled to Africa in 1982 and climbed Mt. Kilimanjaro in a record three days! ✳

The Ewok Wicket, as portrayed by Warwick Davis. "We dared to be cute," admits George Lucas. The Ewoks from the forested moon of Endor were primitive but lovable teddy bears who brought the evil Empire to its metallic knees. African and South Pacific languages were used to create Ewokese, and 134 sketches of the little furballs were generated before Lucas was satisfied with their appearance.

Says William Stout: "For my STAR WARS GALAXY card I chose an art style that goes back nearly to the turn of the century. It was developed by Arthur Rackham, Edmund Dulac and John Bauer. The recipe goes something like this:

"Pencil the drawing and then ink it using a 50/50 solution of India ink and sepia ink. Erase the pencils. Mask off the picture area with tape. Lightly soak the entire picture with an art sponge. While still damp, paint in washes of raw umber watercolor. Use the sponge to take up color in the areas that should remain light or white. This will give the board a slight parchment look.

"Then, begin to build up washes and layers of watercolor. When the coloring is finished, sometimes a little wash here and there of colored inks (never Dr. Martin's dyes — they fade, and some colors photograph strangely) will really perk the colors up and bring back the ink lines as well. Sometimes a little bit of tweaking with Prismacolor pencils brings just the right finishing touch to a piece. Take off the tape, spray with fixative (outside please), and you're done."

GREGTHEAKSTON

"Out of the rocks scurry three Jawas, no taller than Artoo. They holster strange and complex weapons as they cautiously approach the robot. They wear grubby cloaks and their faces are shrouded so that only their glowing yellow eyes can be seen. They hiss and make odd guttural sounds..."

from the "Star Wars" screenplay

"My favorite *Star Wars* memory was taking Ray Harryhausen and Charles Schneer (of the *Sinbad* movies, *Jason and the Argonauts*, *Clash of the Titans*) to see the film on opening day," recalls Greg Theakston. "Together, we watched the new face of fantasy debut."

A lifelong fan of popular culture, Theakston went to work as an illustrator in the early '70s, apprenticing with Jim Steranko. Since then, he's produced over

Jawas were the hooded little hoodlums of *Star Wars* who would beg, borrow (though generally) steal stray droids, then sell them to Tatooine farmers like Luke's Uncle Owen. The Jawas have twinkling eyes set against extremely dark faces, and are never shown with their little hoods off.

250 paperback and magazine illustrations and thousands of commercial storyboards. He currently publishes popular media books, including THE BETTY PAGES and THE WHO'S WHO OF AMERICAN COMIC BOOKS. ✳

Greg Theakston experimented with some Princess Leia concepts before the Jawas piqued his interest. The artist pencils and paints (acrylics) his own creations.

**A
N
G
E
L
O
T
O
R
R
E
S**

"Ewoks in handmade, primitive hanggliders drop rocks onto the stormtroopers. An Imperial Walker lumbers forward, shooting laser blasts at frantic Ewoks running in all directions. Two Ewoks are struck down by laser blasts. One tries to awaken his friend, then realizes that he is dead…"

from the "Return of the Jedi" screenplay

"The *Star Wars* movies continue to be big favorites, to be seen over and over again in my house," says Angelo Torres. "The Han Solo character was something of an Al Williamson space hero come to life. Even now, the imaginative gadgetry still amazes me, so it was fun to be able to draw the Imperial Walker."

Torres served in Korea and upon being discharged in 1953, attended the Cartoonists and Illustrators School (now SVA). Besides comics, he's worked in advertising, magazine illustration, children's books, and has recently finished rendering a 40-page book on the Civil War for Marvel in conjunction with American Heritage, which will be published in the spring of 1994. Torres has also been with MAD MAGAZINE since 1968 and is still relatively sane. ✳

George Lucas: "(The Ewok-Walker battle) evolved out of my interest in a project I was working on at the time that grew out of the Vietnam war, and one of the more fascinating aspects of that project was the human spirit - the human element - being able to withstand an onslaught of high technology. And how the high technology failed…"

"Most of the work I do is in black and white," Angelo Torres explains. "Whenever I am required to work in color, as in the case of this GALAXY card, I am most comfortable using watercolors and color inks over an inked line drawing."

J I M V A L E N T I N O

"Luke stands still, as the Emperor reaches the bottom of the stairs. The Emperor's laughter has turned to anger. He raises his arms toward Luke. Blinding bolts of energy, evil lightning, shoot from the Emperor's hands at Luke. Even in his surprise, the young Jedi tries to use the Force to deflect them…"

from the "Return of the Jedi" screenplay

"Unlike many of the contributors to this series, I was an adult when I first saw *Star Wars*," comments Jim Valentino. I took my stepchildren, and I remember thoroughly enjoying the film — especially since I was seeing it with that youthful sense-of-wonder. Now, years later, my two young sons and I watch the film together on laser disc. It's amazing how cross-generational the *Star Wars* experience is!"

Valentino, one of Image Comics' superstar illustrators, began work in the field back in the late '70s. Accomplishments include NORMALMAN for Aardvark-Vanaheim, animation work for *The Real Ghostbusters* and GUARDIANS OF THE GALAXY (1990) for Marvel. SHADOWHAWK is his recent creation for Image, and SHADOWHAWK III: THROUGH THE PAST DARKLY is an upcoming epic that reveals "what pushed Shadowhawk over the edge," according to its creator. Also upcoming is the ambitious U.S. MALE (written by Valentino, penciled by Murphy Anderson and inked by Mike Allred) and THE PACT, co-written by Valentino and Len Senecal, with art by newcomers Walter McDaniel and Matt Banning. ✱

The Emperor Palpatine strikes down Luke (Mark Hamill) with powerful mind currents at the conclusion of *Return of the Jedi*. Of the Force, George Lucas says: "It's sort of boiling down religion to a very basic concept. The fact that there is some diety, or some power, or some force that sort of controls our destiny, or works for good and also works for evil, has alway been very basic in mankind."

Pen-and-ink guy Jim Valentino reflects on that fiend Palpatine: "The Emperor is a truly fascinating character, an old-line sorcerer in high-tech surroundings. And he raises intriguing questions: is he Luke's grandfather, the first Jedi Knight to fall from grace, like Lucifer? Maybe when George Lucas produces the next trilogy, we'll find out!"

J
O
H
N
V
A
N
F
L
E
E
T

"The Death Star and its Sanctuary Moon hang distant in space as the Rebel fleet comes out of hyperspace with an awesome roar. The Millennium Falcon and several Rebel fighters are at the front as the space armada bears down on its target…"

from the "Return of the Jedi" screenplay

"The kid in me will always remember the sound of a battle taking place in the vacuum of deep space," observes John Van Fleet. "Thanks, George Lucas and Industrial Light and Magic!"

Van Fleet's published works include numerous stories for HELLRAISER as well as a book entitled PRIMAL and several adaptations for THE RAY BRADBURY CHRONICLES. He recently collaborated with writer John

Rieber on a six-part story called SHADOWS FALL for DC's Vertigo line.

The original artwork of much of Van Fleet's creations is regularly on display at New York City's gallery of comic art, Four Color Images. ✳

As the Death Star looms in the background, a Rebel X-wing fighter pursues Darth Vader's TIE fighter in this airbrushed publicity still from *Star Wars*. The spectacular eight-minute "trench" assault on the battle station was accomplished by referring to storyboards designed from watching footage of old, filmed dogfights from World War II. That one sequence took eight weeks to edit.

For both drama and high-tech satisfaction, John Van Fleet rendered two X-wing fighters: the one in the background is presented in its entirety, while the one in the foreground is only partially portrayed — enhancing the sensation of speed (it's racing right off the page!). Van Fleet's finish was accomplished with mixed media, xerography and a belt sander playing important roles in the process.

C
H
A
R
L
E
S

V
E
S
S

"Luke's face is upside-down and showing enormous strain. He stands on his hands, with Yoda perched on his feet. Opposite Luke and Yoda are two rocks the size of bowling balls. Luke stares at the rocks and concentrates. One of the rocks lifts from the ground and floats up to rest on the other..."

from "The Empire Strikes Back" screenplay

"**N**o, I will not do anything with robots in it!" declared Charles Vess when we first approached him for a STAR WARS GALAXY illustration. "Yoda was my favorite character in the trilogy. I like the organic touch of Yoda and the Jungle Planet in *The Empire Strikes Back* that contrasted the hard-edged technological aspect of the rest of the film. As you can tell, I'm not a big fan of technology."

After working a short while in animation, Vess moved to New York City and became an official freelance artist. Some of his early work was for HEAVY METAL and NATIONAL LAM-POON; today he actively contributes to Marvel, DC and Dark Horse comics. Upcoming projects include the magical and mystical ARCANA for DC and a new ALIENS story that's a take-off on "St. George and the Dragon," with a time-warped Alien imper-sonating the old fire-breather. "Okay, so there's technology involved in that story," admits Vess. "But it's Giger-style tech-nology. My kind of meat." ✳

Luke (Mark Hamill) and his teacher Yoda on Dagobah. "George (Lucas) wanted Yoda to talk in a distinctive way and had settled on an inverted style of speaking for the first draft," notes screenwriter Lawrence Kasdan. "I played around with in-version, rhyme, sentences in question form. Finally I found that what I liked best was a repetition of words, a slight inversion that had a medieval tone to it."

As his pencil rough indicates, Charles Vess experimented with composition and mood before coming up with an image that satisfied him. All three visual ingredients — student Luke, teacher Yoda, and the primeval swampscape of Dagobah — were equally important. Vess painted the finish himself, using watercolors.

"The probe droid has spotted Chewbacca who, not thirty feet away, has popped his head over a snow bank. Instantly, the probe robot swings around, its deadly rays ready to fire. But before it can get a shot off, it is hit from behind by a laser bolt, and explodes into a million pieces..."

from "The Empire Strikes Back" screenplay

RUSSELL WALKS

"I owe a debt to George Lucas," admits Russell Walks. "It was he who introduced me to the work of Joseph Campbell, a teacher and philosopher whose wisdom has inspired me to be true to myself and follow my dreams." Walks lives in Montana with his wife and two children. He spends his days drawing, painting, and counting himself lucky that he actually gets paid for doing what he loves.

Since his foray into the STAR WARS GALAXY for Topps, the artist has ventured into another facet of the Lucasfilm Universe. He is currently working on two different Indiana Jones adventures for Dark Horse Comics: INDIANA JONES AND THE GOLDEN FLEECE, a two-part micro-series, and the four-issue INDIANA JONES AND THE ARMS OF GOLD. Walks also painted the cover for DC's trade paperback THE BEST OF STAR TREK: THE NEXT GENERATION, as well as the interior art for Open Court Publishing's adaptation of Ray Bradbury's THE FOG HORN.

Peter Mayhew as Chewbacca, the towering, 200-year old Wookiee. George Lucas has a special fondness for this character, since it was derived from his pet, a malamute dog named Indiana. He was a very large, furry animal who looked like the Wookiee - only smaller. David Prowse was originally offered the role of Chewbacca, but decided to play Darth Vader instead.

"Although I've always enjoyed the *Star Wars* trilogy on an escapist level,' reflects Walks, "I think part of its appeal runs deeper. *Star Wars* is about more than laser blasts and lightsabers. It is about redemption. And friendship. And it's about the quest for meaning and understanding that we all undertake at some point in our lives. These are the emotions and ideas that strike a chord in me. And they are responsible for making *Star Wars* more than just a cool collection of special effects." ✶

Russell Walks works with watercolor and colored pencil on "hot press" paper, which has a smooth finish and is designed to hold water without buckling.

AL WILLIAMSON

"Stormtroopers hurriedly set up a large bazookalike weapon. Behind them the giant hangar door opens slowly. A laser gun appears on the Falcon and swings around to aim at the Imperial troops. The stormtroopers, preparing to fire their bazooka cannon, are hit by the Falcon's fire and are thrown about in all directions."

from "The Empire Strikes Back" screenplay

"I always liked the characters of *Star Wars*," recalls Al Williamson. "They were very real, very human. And the creatures that inhabited this universe were a helluva lot of fun to draw. I took certain liberties with the Dewback lizard — mine was sleeker, more streamlined than George's"

Known for his elegant line, veteran illustrator Williamson is no stranger to George Lucas' stellar creation: he rendered both THE EMPIRE STRIKES BACK and RETURN OF THE JEDI adaptations for Marvel and spent over three years on the STAR WARS newspaper strip (recently reprinted — with new Williamson covers — for Dark Horse).

It was back in 1949 that Al Williamson began his career with JOHN WAYNE COMICS for Toby Press, Al Capp's company. Memorable science fiction stories for EC followed, along with Timely westerns. A longtime admirer of Alex Raymond's elegant, swashbuckling creations, Williamson rendered the FLASH GORDON newspaper strip ('66 - '67) for King Features as well as the enduring SECRET AGENT X-9.

Recently, Williamson returned to his science fiction roots by rendering scenes from the 1955 movie classic *This Island Earth* for Topps' UNIVERSAL MONSTERS card set.

Al Williamson contributed two images to the STAR WARS GALAXY card set: the aforementioned Dewback lizard (complete with saddled stormtrooper) and a pair of Imperial snowtroopers, featured in *The Empire Strikes Back*. Williamson's inked linework has dazzled comic book enthusiasts for decades. ✳

The Imperial stormtroopers, helmeted, armor-clad soldiers who live (and frequently die) for the Empire, must accustom themselves to extreme temperatures, as they are sent all over the galaxy in search of Rebels and their hidden bases. In *Star Wars*, a stormtrooper patrols the Tatooine desert on the back of a monstrous Dewback lizard; in *The Empire Strikes Back*, "snowtroopers" fight the icy chill by heating things up for Princess Leia and her companions.

THOMAS M. YEATES

"Luke hesitates only a moment… On his homeworld of Tatooine he's ridden everything from Banthas to Dewback lizards. How bad can this be? Leaping upon the winged creature…he immediately finds out!"

from the newspaper comic strip

"The *Star Wars* movie trilogy was important to me not only because it was a stunning experience," concludes Tom Yeates, "but because it encouraged revolution during an otherwise repressive era."

Yeates is known for drawing characters in wild, non-urban settings. He rendered short stories for SGT. ROCK, MYSTERY IN SPACE, GHOSTS and other DC series before landing his first regular job, the revival of SWAMP THING (1982).

Since '86 he's contributed to SCOUT, AIRBOY, LUGER, ALIEN WORLDS, REAL WAR STORIES, BROUGHT TO LIGHT (a controversial graphic novel from Eclipse) and Topps' DRACULA VERSUS. ZORRO .

Currently, Yeates is rendering TARZAN for Dark Horse — and loving every minute of it. Also on his agenda is Epic's TIME SPIRITS. ✳

In *Return of the Jedi*, Luke Skywalker (Mark Hamill) emerges as a full-fledged Jedi Knight, confident of his powers, mindful of his responsibilites. "Luke Skywalker is the straight line through *Star Wars*," explains Hamill. "He's the one you're always watching." The saga is actually a coming-of-age story, with Luke growing up before our eyes over the course of three films.

Tom Yeates sent his preliminary roughs to headquarters and suggested a horizontal treatment of the flying serpent scene. Topps' creative staff preferred the vertical approach.

THE ART OF STAR WARS GALAXY

EVERYONE COMES TO THE CANTINA

"The murky, moldy den is filled with a startling array of weird and exotic alien creatures and monsters at the long metallic bar. At first the sight is horrifying. One-eyed, thousand- eyed, slimy, furry, scaly, tentacled, and clawed creatures huddle over drinks…"

from the "Star Wars" screenplay

"The cantina scene," Bruce Zick observes, "is the threshold moment of transition into a fabulous and daring world of fantasy, imagination and sense of wonder. It's that step through the looking glass that Alice once dared to take, the one moment that changes our perception of reality. When Luke and Obi-Wan stepped into the cantina, not only did *Star Wars* take a quantum leap forward, but the future of film art direction was redefined, and the imagination of a world-wide audience bolted into a brave new frontier."

Zick is a man of many talents. Gourmet, sign painter, engineer and radio DJ, he's also lent his creative skills to motion pictures and TV programs. Comics work includes ARGOSY and TERMINAL POINT for Dark Horse, THOR, PIRATES OF DARKWATER and SLEEPWALKER for Marvel.

Upcoming series include ATLAS and THE PECULIAR ADVENTURES OF NORMAN VAN NOSTRUM (both Dark Horse, 1994) and the return of the critically-acclaimed ZONE CONTINUUM for Caliber Press. ✳

B
R
U
C
E
Z
I
C
K

Explains Bruce Zick: "I wanted to convey as much information as possible without sacrificing clarity and message so I chose a deep-focus shot of three spatial planes, also known as mise-en-scene. A strong close-up look at detailed faces, placement of secondary characters, sense of atmosphere, and a story moment of Luke's spotlit entrance were all combined in one shot."

Everyone loved the cantina sequence from the first *Star Wars*…except George Lucas, who felt it could be better. "(Stuart Freeborn) designed Chewbacca and several of the creatures for the cantina," expains producer Gary Kurtz. "He fell ill, though, before we got that sequence finished, and had to leave the picture and go to the hospital for eight weeks." *Return of the Jedi* provided Lucas with an opportunity to improve upon the concept with more sophisticated make-up and special effects.

A SNEAK PREVIEW

TOPPS' STAR WARS GALAXY Series 2 trading cards will be available in early spring, 1994. This follow-up series will feature an expanded "New Visions" sub-set offering all-new art by all-new artists. Among these creations is this original take on the fearsome Tusken Raiders of Tatooine, as illustrated by Tim Truman.